TO THE SILENCED
AN DIE VERSTUMMTEN

Georg Trakl

TO THE SILENCED
AN DIE VERSTUMMTEN

SELECTED POEMS

TRANSLATED AND INTRODUCED
BY
WILL STONE

2005

Published by Arc Publications,
Nanholme Mill, Shaw Wood Road
Todmorden OL14 6DA, UK

Copyright in original poems
© Trakl Haus Foundation 2005
and © Brenner-Archiv 2005
Translation copyright © Will Stone, 2005
Introduction copyright © Will Stone, 2005

Design by Tony Ward
Cover design by Tony Ward
Printed and bound in the UK by Lightning Source

ISBN-13: 978 1 904614 10 4
ISBN-10: 1 904614 10 8

The publishers wish to thank: Forschungsinstitut Brenner-Archiv,
Innsbruck for permission to reproduce: 'Ex Libris' Georg Trakl
by Max v. Esterle on the cover; Georg Trakl Caricature by Max
v. Esterle on p. 10; Georg Trakl at the Lido, Venice, photograph,
August 1913 on p. 21; the last poems 'Klage' and 'Grodek' written
on the reverse of 'Testaments Brief', Trakl's letter to Ficker,
Krakow, 27 October 1914 on p 32; and the Georg-Trakl-
Forschungs-und-Gedenkstätte, Salzburg for permission to re-
produce Georg Trakl photograph, May 1914 on p. 162. The pub-
lishers also wish to thank Will Stone for allowing them to use his
photographs taken during the preparation of this book.

The publishers acknowledge financial assistance
from ACE Yorkshire

Arc Publications Translation Series
Editor: Jean Boase-Beier

To my parents

Acknowledgements

I am grateful to the editors of the following journals in which a number of my Trakl translations first appeared. *Modern Poetry in Translation, Pretext, The International Review* and *Poetry Salzburg*. I would also like to thank Arts Council East for their financial contribution towards this project and the British Centre for Literary Translation who granted me a period as Translator in Residence at the University of East Anglia to work on these translations.

I would like to give generous thanks to those individuals without whose help this book would not have come to fruition. Firstly I acknowledge the enthusiasm and generous assistance shown me by Dr Hans Weichselbaum at the Trakl Haus foundation and archive in Salzburg. His permission to use photographs and illustrations from the collection is gratefully appreciated, as was his willingness to act as guide to sites of special interest in Salzburg relating to the poet. Thanks also to Professor Eberhard Sauermann for allowing me to view original manuscripts, letters and photographs at the Brenner Archive in Innsbruck. Here in the UK my heartfelt thanks go to Arc's tireless editor Dr Jean Boase-Beier for her steadfast support, her wise editorial input and personal commitment to these translations. Lastly I would like to take this opportunity to acknowledge the legacy of the poet Michael Hamburger, whose literary contribution to this country in the course of the last sixty years is immeasurable and who first landed Trakl on anglophone shores in the form of a little known pamphlet of twelve poems published by The Latin Press, St Ives over half a century ago.

Will Stone

CONTENTS

Translator's Preface / 11
Revelation and Downfall:
An Introduction to Georg Trakl / 17
Part I – Life / 17
Part II – Work / 24
Part III – Further Reading / 34

SELECTED POEMS

Georg Trakl caricature by Max v. Esterle
© Brenner-Archiv

TRANSLATOR'S PREFACE

By the late autumn of 2001, I had completed the better part of these translations. A number of poems were beginning to take their first tentative steps in sympathetic journals but I had still not secured a publisher. I was however reasonably upbeat. There had not been a new book of Trakl's poetry for decades. The pioneering Sixties Press collection by Bly/Wright in the US had been followed in 1968 by Cape's dark green pocket book of translations by Michael Hamburger, Christopher Middleton and others. It was largely these versions which solidified Trakl's reputation in the UK as a key European poet. This Cape book is now a collector's item and is increasingly hard to find. But for years Trakl's works have been out of print and despite a repackage of the Hamburger book in the eighties from Carcanet, including letters and prose poems, though sadly no German, there had been nothing since in the UK and to my mind Trakl seemed in desperate need of a reappraisal. I also noticed how the French were stacking Trakl on tables in their bookshops in a handsome new Gallimard edition, whereas here poets of Trakl's calibre were customarily incarcerated in some unvisited corner at the back of the shop where the occasional flutter of their flag of genius wouldn't deflect anyone already marooned in the spreading pool of lurid fiction at the entrance. However, by sheer coincidence another rival Trakl book had loomed up out of nowhere and was about to be published. There was nothing I could do but pull back and presumably wait a few years, though I knew that my book had a different approach and that the two could easily exist simultaneously. To make matters worse a collection from Anvil, a mysterious spectre, haunted the imagination of prospective publishers. This book, which has never materialised in physical form but appears on Amazon and other lists as if it is just about to, made my task even more futile.

Following such traumas, the Trakl project slid wearily

11

into the sidings for a few more years and other challenges presented themselves. But then in a second attempt to secure a berth I had the good fortune to find support from Arc and together we have been able to finally present these new translations as a generous 'Selected Poems' in which the majority of key works are represented. I have tried to present the poems in roughly chronological order, following the titles of those collections in the German from which they are extracted. The objective has always been to provide the core of Trakl's poetry in a bilingual edition, presenting all the most powerful and famous poems as well as others of considerable worth which are more obscure. To this aim I have included a higher density of poems from the middle to latter stages of Trakl's career, though some of the more interesting and distinctive early poems are also given a well-deserved airing. I felt it was counter-productive to readers, especially those new to Trakl, to swamp them with every single poem he produced and with some even in multiple versions, though I accept such an approach is of value. I wanted rather to hit the reader with the full force of Trakl's vision without any peripheral padding, to create something more streamlined that packed a definite punch, rather than be content with a vague swing through the air.

After much deliberation I have not included the prose poems here either, partly due to lack of space but also because I wanted to maintain the momentum of the verse translations. The prose poems certainly contain some impressive imagery, particularly in 'Dream and Derangement', but they lack the decisive pauses and more honed feeling of the verse poems, which gives the sense of their holding a spring-coiled visionary energy gathered in the least number of words necessary to contain it. This is especially evident in the later poems. Sometimes in the prose poems the images seem clogged and rather overblown as if one is suffocating another. They tend to run down the page in a cascade of delirium into which one gropes excitedly for an anchor only to find more of the same. The limited space of the verse poem, the invisible shape within which the poem fits works to maximise Trakl's visionary impulse, selects more of the red meat so to speak and strips away the fat.

This collection, then, is not an exhaustive scholarly tome, neither is it a 'Greatest Hits' of Trakl, but I hope a representative selection which delivers the poems with as little erosion to their vision as is possible given the limits of translation. I wanted to produce a reader-friendly, accessible and with luck even durable edition which could be accessed by anyone interested in poetry and at reasonable cost. It is high time Trakl was released from the rather narrow confines of German-language academia and was given the opportunity to appeal to a more diverse readership as is the case with his Gallic forebear Rimbaud. Having once attended a Trakl literary event I was dismayed to observe that everyone in the room bar myself and the girl struggling with a tray of canapés was in late middle age and of academic extraction. If this had been a reading of Rimbaud's poetry, the audience would surely have reflected a much more healthy cross-section of ages and backgrounds. Rimbaud is of course an icon like Dylan Thomas or for that matter Bob Dylan. His reach goes far beyond the domain of the literary world. Given the 'difficult' hermetical nature of his poetic language and (in spite of an unrivalled visionary intensity) the limited range, Trakl is hardly likely to join these reluctant deities, but I sense there are many more people who would be deeply rewarded by discovering his work if they actually knew of his existence.

I have to confess I have avoided most of the formally rhymed early poems. These lesser works do not lend themselves easily to translation nor are they the most deserving of inclusion. I feel more comfortable translating from free verse forms, since that is the form which my creative English seems to favour in my own work. As a translator of poetry I must in the end have a real poem to show for my struggle, not a collection of carefully constructed lines which read like a poem but are in fact already decomposing before they reach the page. It doesn't always come off, but if there are more that succeed than fail then one carries on. I try to let a new poem create itself from the ingredients which the original has left over in the cupboard. One can be creative with very little when cooking. I never construct something in a painstakingly over-conscious manner. I do not approach translation like a *Telegraph* crossword, nor do I like to embroider in order to whip up the orchestra. Music comes from the new poem's identity, its unique pulse. People talk about retaining the music of the original as if somehow the melody can be re-wired. Music cannot be 'reconstructed' out of old notes torn out of their native soil and somehow rearranged. Slapping on more and more filler will never make the repair look convincing. The only way is to go back to the bare metal. I am concerned with borrowing Trakl from the German language. Is that all? No. It just happens that this was the language Trakl was born into. I am instead trying to absorb and filter that more elusive language lying just beyond, a language which the German is privileged to carry. The German is where the poetry breathes freely and it does not suffer fools gladly. In trying to wrench Trakl out without due care, one may inadvertently tickle the toe of a monster. Language has a nasty habit of obscuring our thoughts at the moment when *it* becomes the subject. The religious leader Rowan Williams is perhaps an unlikely figure to wheel on here, but he seems to have grasped something of this which he expresses in a refreshingly simple way. "If a translator catches the music, not of the words which is impossible to reproduce, but of the 'symmetric' complexes of image and feeling, what emerges is still poetry.

Much has been said about the translation of poetry and it remains a fiercely subjective battlefield where two opposing sides representing freedom and fidelity periodically slug it out. One usually finds oneself wandering somewhere between the two in no-mans land trying to win the approval of both sides. This is generally where the most readable and comfortable translations spring up, Stephen Mitchell's *Rilke*, let us say, or Anthony Hasler's

14

Heym. Even the *Baudelaire* and *Rimbaud* of Messrs Scarfe and Bernard, interestingly two of the most enduring prose translations of major European poets, stake out this liberal ground. That's not to say the extremes don't have their value, but they tire easily since they make a lot more noise. The general reader expects consistency and faithfulness to the original 'voice' of the poetry. He / she needs to trust the translator. How many times does one hear the complaint that somehow the reader suspects he / she is getting a raw deal, that the original is diluted and the poet's voice is coming through watered down or disabled in some way, that the apprentice has tried to out-perform the master. In the situation where a reader does not know the original language they tend to go with how the English sounds as a poem; what else can they do? Mitchell's *Rilke* for example arguably sounds a whole lot better to the ear than Walter Arndt's versions, which are religiously faithful to the original structure. In order to achieve this fidelity Arndt must shoehorn rhymes in again and again which sound forced and unnatural. Arndt however has lambasted Mitchell for being 'inaccurate' and taking liberties. In order to get where he wants to go in terms of fluency, Mitchell has to embroider a little, he has to squeeze a bit of paste in here and there to seal the holes, but not so much that he veers off course. He achieves a balance and makes a sound enough judgement. He makes the best of what he has. The charge of 'inaccuracy' could equally be levelled at those translators who fail to translate the language behind the original language, which as suggested earlier, is merely a vehicle for the poetic impulse which one is trying to connect with and bring across intact. Without the support of this elusive voice it doesn't matter how accurate one is, the result will always be stillborn.

Literary translation is a resiliently complex process which is still far from being understood despite the groaning weight of academic texts on the discipline itself. There will always be the same tedious arguments on questions of freedom and fidelity, a see-saw which has been so long locked into placating both its opposing poles it seems to have found its own back and forth momentum. Surely little more needs to be said. There are however a few basic necessities one must take on board, such as the ability to raid with impunity the linguistic store house of one's native language, to 'enable' the mother tongue and make use of all the stylistic devices available in order to quell the ravenous appetite for 'compensation'. For those who are not accustomed to these dreary translation terms, that is to make up for what is lost from the source language, such as a formal rhyme scheme for example. However, surely the main thing on any translator's mind is not to leave to posterity something which would act as a gross impediment to the original poem, which after all gave it life. How many great poets must endure a line of mumbling delinquents trudging behind them all claiming to be their true friend and representative in a foreign tongue? For my part I can only hope that these new translations do not act as an encumbrance and will help contribute to that full freedom of movement Trakl deserves in the English language.

Will Stone

REVELATION AND DOWNFALL:
AN INTRODUCTION TO GEORG TRAKL

It is not my intention in this essay to enter into an in-depth study of individual Trakl poems, nor to leave my footprints on the well-trodden paths which lead to those inevitable snares of incest, psychopathology, schizophrenia or religious signification, which continue to obsess Trakl scholars. My aim is to provide an accessible introduction for both newcomers to Trakl and old hands who may need reminding. I should like merely to provide the basic tools necessary to explore the poems in my translation and furnish the reader with some background information which I hope will make their excursion into this new territory a rewarding one. For those Anglophone readers who require more detailed analysis, I recommend that they consult the list of publications cited at the end of this section. For a sound critical reading of the poetry one might acquire for example *The Poet's Madness – A Reading of Georg Trakl's Poetry* by Francis Michael Sharpe, whilst on themes such as death and incest *Georg Trakl's Poetry – Towards a Union of Opposites* by Richard Detsch makes a valuable contribution. Maire Kurrik's brief but perceptive account on the relationship between Trakl's mental state and his poetry is also worth seeking out, as are Herbert Lindenberger's 'Profile' in the Twayne series and of course Michael Hamburger's valuable essay from his collection on German literature 'Reason and Energy' (1957).

Part i – Life

Georg Trakl was born on 3 February 1887 to Tobias and Maria Trakl, a comfortably-off bourgeois Salzburg family, whose wealth came from a profitable hardware business. Early photographs show the young Georg posing dutifully with his five brothers and sisters for the family album. Georg was the third youngest of the Trakl siblings. After him came his brother Fritz and sister Grete the youngest, who would become such a significant fig-

17

ure in both his life and the later interpretation of his poetry, due primarily to the physical and emotional longing they held for each other and the subsequent torment over such a sinful union suffered by the poet. These early snapshots appear to have been taken on family days out, perhaps to fairgrounds and carnivals. One shows Georg as a boy of about ten leaning on the window ledge of a fake log cabin, flanked by his uncle and brother Fritz. This is a commercial photographer's set, steeped in touristic Tyrolean kitsch and the young Georg suitably exhibits an air of indifference. Another popular pose was to have all the children seated in rowing fashion on the floor in the order of their years, or to dress them all identically in the ubiquitous sailor suits. Given what we know of Trakl's background, these formal images of an unremarkable prosperous middle class family simply recording their days of leisure in and around their native city are somehow unsettling in their deliberate attempt to show normality, when behind the façade familial dysfunction was already flourishing.

From the outset young Georg showed signs of mental instability. His parents were often distant and absorbed in their own affairs. The stifling bourgeois atmosphere of suppressed anxieties and thwarted passions created fertile ground for the flowering of psychopathology and social alienation. Several alarming accounts of suicidal impulse come through from Trakl's childhood. Around the age of six or seven it is alleged that he walked fully-clothed into a pond until just his hat was resting on the surface. Luckily he was spotted and fished out just in time. On another occasion he threw himself without warning before some race horses but escaped injury and on another he leapt out before a moving train.

From an early age he complained of visual hallucinations and being pestered by the ringing of bells. As a youth he would imbibe chloroform and dip his cigarettes in opium. A life-long taste for narcotics was established. He was also a heavy drinker; taverns and drunkenness feature widely in his poetry. Trakl's mammoth consumption of drugs and alcohol was legendary amongst his circle. This addiction was due in part to youthful rebellion and the craving for bohemian excess as well as a nod to Rimbaud's notorious clarion call for the 'poète maudit' to seek a 'derangement of the senses' in order to achieve visionary states. However, as time went on Trakl relied more and more on his intake of drugs as a desperate shield against reality and particularly the abject failure he sensed in his own personal life, feelings only intensified by existential over-stimulation. Witnesses tell of the youthful Trakl's penchant for launching into prolonged drunken monologues in local taverns. He often visited prostitutes too but more often than not would just talk on in those characteristic monosyllabic tones, the romantic outsider expressing his affinity with their noble position as social outlaws.

Early literary signs were displayed in his joining the bohemian literary group 'Apollo', later renamed 'Minerva'. Trakl eagerly devoured Baudelaire and Verlaine in translation, read Nietzsche and Dostoyevsky avidly. Dostoyevsky's collected works became his prized possession, which he was forced to sell later with much regret in order to escape penury. Initial attempts to publish his work ended in disaster. Some early attempts at drama were summarily given the *coup de grace* by their author after being raked with critical fire. But by now Trakl was living the life of a fully-fledged bohemian artist and had, as the doctrine demanded, become estranged from his whole family save for Grete, his younger sister, whom he idealised and worshipped and with whom he suffered the mutual guilt of the blackest sin of all, incest. Whether the incestuous act which so obsesses Trakl scholars actually took place or was just a wilful desire on both sides has not been firmly established. However, the impact of the guilt of this liaison on Trakl's psychology is of paramount importance. But incest aside, it is clear that Trakl still held a deep and lifelong affection for a younger sister whose own anxieties, passions and eccentric behaviour he could easily identify with and until the end of their brief lives they remained unquestionably devoted to each other.

In 1905, Trakl began work as an apprentice pharmacist at 'The White Angel' pharmacy on the Linzergasse in Salzburg. This was a position well suited to his needs and he was able to experiment with a range of drugs and discover those which gave the most effective relief, albeit temporary, from morbid anxiety and social phobia. In 1908 he moved to Vienna to commence his studies at University. This period in the capital brought about a near breakdown as Trakl moved restlessly about the city, a virtual itinerant, oppressed by the stifling air of moral and cultural deterioration, the 'whipped cream' bourgeois superficiality of the metropolis. He describes these difficult months in a letter as 'days of raving drunkenness and criminal melancholy...' Though Trakl had soft words for Salzburg at times, more often than not it too felt the venom of his tongue, as later did Innsbruck. Trakl's hypersensitivity and fear of crowds tended to encourage a heightened sense of metrophobia, whilst those more natural surroundings which tend to nourish the solitary such as woods, parklands and ancient cemeteries provided a temporary respite.

In 1910 Tobias Trakl died quite suddenly after an illness and Trakl was left starved of the usual allowance. His financial situation fell rapidly into disarray causing yet more anguish and insecurity. After graduating he was obliged to spend a year in the army, not an altogether unpleasant time, since being of middle-class stock he was saved from the most menial and intolerable duties. Afterwards, seeking employment, he attempted a return to 'The White Angel' but without success. Trakl's growing incapacity to socially interact, an aberration aggravated by self-loathing of his physical appearance, was a severe impediment to holding such a position. He then drifted between the major Austrian cities, penniless and bereft of hope. It seemed that this lonely figure was doomed to fade away in the anonymity of the metropolis, just another vagrant's corpse to be peered at through the windows of the city morgue.

Fortunately, a sudden move to Innsbruck in 1912 and a lucky break at the military pharmacy there propelled him into a crucial meeting with the man who would become both saviour and friend as well as his loyal and committed publisher. Ludwig von Ficker was the editor of the influential literary magazine *Der Brenner*. He befriended the shy, withdrawn poet from Salzburg and quickly realised on reading his poems that he possessed a unique and extraordinary talent. This first reading was the trigger for Trakl's swift ascendancy to influential European poet. For the next two years Ficker took on the role of guardian and father-figure to Trakl, encouraging and supporting him while he began to write the mature works on which his fame now rests. Not a single issue of *Der Brenner* appeared without a significant contribution from Trakl. His first full-length collection appeared in 1913, entitled simply *Poems*. A second, *Sebastian in Dream* was soon planned to follow, but only appeared after his death. Reassured by Ficker's loyal support and admiration, Trakl produced a flood of new, more powerful and

Georg Trakl at the Lido, Venice, August 1913

accomplished poems from 1913 through 1914. Ficker also introduced Trakl to other important poets and writers of the era such as Else Lasker-Schüler and Karl Kraus. Trakl acknowledged these new acquaintances and admirers by dedicating certain poems to them. In the summer of 1913, Trakl accompanied Ficker and Kraus on a rare vacation to Venice. A remarkable photo shows the poet standing out in dark bathing costume against the pale sands of the lido. He is holding something in his hand and appears to be weighing it up. Even under a magnifying glass it is impossible to be sure what this tantalisingly obscure object is, a shell, a coin, the stub of a cigarette? He appears utterly incongruous to his surroundings, as if superimposed on the background, despite the fact that he is appropriately dressed for the environment. In a later poem he refers to Venice as the ante-room to hell.

In March 1914 Grete Trakl became seriously ill and Georg dutifully hurried to her bedside. She survived for now at least, only to take her life some three years later during a final bout of suicidal depression. Excusing herself from a party one evening she left the room and then shot herself. It was said that she found it unbearable to live having failed to come to terms with the death of her beloved brother. It was around this time that Trakl met the German Jewish poet Else Lasker-Schüler to whom he dedicated the poem 'The West'. During the summer of 1914 the philosopher Ludwig Wittgenstein decided to allot a considerable sum of money to deserving poets writing in the German language. Ficker was given the task of choosing those he felt most worthy of such a windfall. Trakl was one of the principal recipients, as was Rilke. The latter collected his reward without undue difficulty, but Trakl, who was desperately short of resources, failed to even get his hands on the money. Overwhelmed by the prospect of dealing with strangers at the bank, he suffered an attack of acute anxiety en route and, drenched in perspiration, fled in terror.

War now loomed and in the initial wave of ill-starred euphoria and patriotism, Trakl was conscripted as a medical orderly in the Austrian army. His unit was promptly despatched to Galicia. Following the carnage at the battle of Grodek, a place immortalised in the famous poem of that name, Trakl was obliged to care for some ninety wounded soldiers in a barn behind the lines. Lacking sufficient medical supplies to care for the men adequately, he could do little but witness their suffering. Tormented by the wailing and groaning of the wounded, Trakl suffered an attack of panic, then to make matters worse one man ended his misery by shooting himself in the head. Seeing his brains splattered on the wall, Trakl broke down completely. He fled the barn only to see the bodies of executed deserters swinging from the trees. One horror piled on top of another. This fatal surge of bestial realities had smashed through Trakl's precarious mental defences. A few days later, he stood up abruptly at the meal table and calmly announced to his comrades that he was about to shoot himself. He was overpowered and relieved of his post. His destination was the military hospital at Krakow where he was placed in a cell and detained for observation. Psychiatrists soon diagnosed *Dementia Praecox* or as we know it today schizophrenia. Ficker rushed from Innsbruck to his friend's aid, knowing that Trakl would be unable to endure such a hostile environment for long. Ficker arrived on 3 November and tried desperately to secure Trakl's release but without immediate success. Ficker's fears over his friend's mental state were duly confirmed when the night after he left Trakl took an overdose of cocaine acquired from a guard he had befriended and was found dead next morning in his cell. His remains were buried in the grounds of the military hospital and remained there until 1925 when, after Ficker's intervention, they were moved to the cemetery near his home at the village of Mühlau on the edge of Innsbruck. Ficker himself lived until 1967 and on his death requested that his remains be buried next to those of his friend. Poet

and publisher now lie side by side in perpetuity beneath the delicate spread of a miniature silver birch.

Trakl's grave

23

'Who could he have been?' asked Rainer Maria Rilke of the author of a long poem (entitled 'Sebastian in Dream') by which he had just been overwhelmed. Rilke was one of a growing number of admirers of the Salzburg poet who were becoming ever more aware of the significance of this unique voice in German language poetry, a voice speaking a provocative and wholly entrancing new language of arcane dream, spectral shrouded myth and fleeting symbol, a voice both brutally insistent and painfully fragile which seemed to have left the majority of those who heard it fumbling confusedly in its wake. Trakl, an unwavering romantic and solitary figure appeared to have sunk so deep inside himself that he was creating a new visionary language all his own; a language that dispensed a complexity of images both beguiling and unsettling to confound and captivate readers in equal measure.

With his customary tendency to articulate inwardness, Rilke alone seemed perfectly poised to interpret the elusive quality of the Trakl poem. In a letter of 1917 to Erhard Buschbeck, Trakl's lifelong friend, Rilke sought to define the enigma surrounding the poetry:

> For me, the Trakl poem is an object of sublime existence… but now it puzzles me how its form, fleeting from the start and delicately by-passed in description, could possibly bear the weight of its eternal oblivion in such precise images.

Two years earlier in a letter of 1915, just after Trakl's death in Krakow, he had written to Ficker:

> …I have discovered much in them: overwhelmed, amazed, wondering and mystified; for one soon realises that the conditions of these tones which rise and fall away are irrevocably singular, like those circumstances in which a dream might arise. I imagine that even one who is stood close by must experience such spectacles and perceptions as though pressed, an exile, against a pane of glass: for Trakl's life passes as if through the images of a

mirror and fills its entire space, which cannot be entered, like the space of the mirror itself.'

Trakl's poetry habitually leaves critics chasing their tails. This is hardly surprising. It has been said more than once that to absorb and interpret the visionary essence of Trakl's poetry readers would have to be in a virtual state of delirium themselves. There is perhaps an element of truth to this somewhat controversial claim; one can't help thinking that the Trakl poem may require a certain melancholic, even pathological, propensity in the reader to permit the infection proper of what one might call the 'sympathetic imagination'. Conventional language has here been rejected in favour of one which better expresses interiority. Seemingly incoherent cascades of images combine to infest the imagination of the reader and steadfastly deny the intrusion of rationality. The marriage of hallucinatory and dream-like visions with real, lived experience and personal dysfunction creates indefinable scenes of corrupted innocence and apocalyptic turbulence where the unconscious has been mobilized to check the advance of an evil external world which the poet's fragile self finds insupportable. This dream language, for want of a better word, is admittedly a product of schizophrenia, evolving to its most exotic state in poets like Trakl and Hölderlin.

Karl Jaspers, in his seminal study of Strindberg and Van Gogh, but in particular thinking of Hölderlin, discusses the delusions and hallucinations produced by the schizophrenic mind, words that could equally be applied to Trakl.

> Just as a diseased oyster causes the formation of pearls, schizophrenic processes can bring about the formation of unique spiritual works. One who experiences the power of works which to them generate life thinks of schizophrenia, which may have been one of the conditions of their creation, no more than one who takes pleasure from the pearl thinks of the oyster's sickness. Yet those who crave understanding demand genesis and circumstances and there is no limit to their questioning.

This poignant statement look forwards to the futile search for meaning in Trakl's poetry by scholars ensnared by their own agendas. There is no doubt that the nature of Trakl's poetry was heavily influenced by his mental disease. Jaspers again points eerily to Trakl when he goes on to say: 'One observes how schizophrenics form their own mythology, which for them exists self-evidently and unquestionably, and which often adopts this timeless quality.'

The overwhelming pressures of existential alienation, failure in love, self-loathing and religious torment, not to mention the ever-present spectre of incest, are the individual rocks gradually piled onto Trakl's chest, a load which only gets heavier as his life goes on. If he is not to be finally crushed he must attain a form of transcendence, he must part either spiritually or physically from the pestilent body which he senses is infecting the once pure and untainted divinity of childhood. In a letter from Salzburg in the summer of 1913 he writes the following caustic lines:

> I long for the day when the soul neither will nor can live any longer in this unholy body blighted by melancholy, that the soul will depart this absurd body formed of filth and decay – a body which is only an all too true reflection of a godless and accursed century.

Also present is the wider sense of generational decline and mankind's impulsion towards extinction having utterly forsaken the nobleness and purity of that divine path symbolised for Trakl in the hymnic poetry of Hölderlin. Such fears of irreversible decline only spread the apocalyptic blaze. The mouldering away of the Hapsburg Empire and the spiritual vacuousness flaunted by an increasingly mercantile metropolitan society in the run-up to war can only have intensified the atmosphere of corruption and decay. In response Trakl delivers an anachronistic rural landscape, a medieval world of lost shepherds, monks, singers and saints, figures who only serve to exacerbate the illusory and enchanted domain in which his poems are set. Mournful scenes of threatened innocence endlessly repeat or reappear ghost-like in another form.

Colours abound with the most indecipherable and ambiguous associations, in spite of Heidegger's infamous claim that a comprehensible symbolic code existed. Following any rationale regarding the use of colour in the Trakl poem can prove treacherous. Everywhere in these poems colours predominate. Some seem firmly anchored to their image whilst others appear as if added somewhat arbitrarily like dabs of paint to an almost finished canvas. Trakl often returned to his poems again and again to make changes so one cannot be sure whether certain colours were there from the outset or added later. It is not surprising, then, that Trakl's poetry has often been likened to the impressionistic method of painting where colours combine according to the caprice of the painterly eye to create a particular atmosphere, mood or tone. This use of colour as a means of modulating the expressive power of an image (whether symbolic, realistic or merely as an unconscious impulse) is crucial to the power and impact of the overall poem. Removing the colour from a Trakl poem would be like silencing the entire wind or string section of an orchestra in mid flow.

Sometimes the same colour appears again and again, even in the same poem. Blue is perhaps the most dominant and is generally thought to represent purity and silence, calmness and peace. Blue or blueness is often applied to emphasise the sanctity of nature in both the landscape and its inhabitants, as yet untainted by mankind: 'A blue deer', 'A blue flower's holiness', 'The blue brows of the fathers', 'A pure blue steps from a shell decayed'. Although the blue applied may often be symbolic, it could also be merely realistic: 'a blue river' or 'a blue pond'. The other shades and colours seem still more ambiguous – white, black and green are also heavily employed and to a lesser extent, red, gold, yellow, grey and brown – but any further attempt at explaining the use of these colours is clearly futile. The colours are best left where they are, in poetic flux; their passage from inwardness to the poem should not be obstructed by any craving for explication.

It is interesting to compare the colour symbolism of Trakl to much of the over-consciously elaborated *fin de siècle* poetry of the previous century which also drew heavily on colour. Much of this now appears dated and somewhat contrived. In the hand of Trakl, however, such an approach appears remarkably free of affectation. The unique musical qualities of Trakl's poetry enhanced by the use of colour have not been lost on generations of composers who have sought to create musical scores based on his poems. These range from well-known figures like Webern, Hindemith and Knussen to lesser-known names such as Michael Graubart, Leopold Spinner and Wolfgang Rihm, with more recent experiments from composers Pawel Szymanski, Thea Musgrave and Christopher Rouse. Webern's six songs op. 14 to Georg Trakl is the best known, and includes pieces for 'The Sun', 'The West' and 'Song of a captive blackbird'. It is, however, the composer Alban Berg who would, to my mind, appear the most likely candidate to have drawn on Trakl, since his music seems closest of all in mood to the imagery of the poetry, but interestingly, he did not..

Mysterious personae are constructed such as 'Elis', 'Helian' and 'Sebastian', or even the more easily identified 'Kaspar Hauser'. These solitary souls, poised to endure decline (and presumably annihilation), still radiate, sharing both Trakl's own afflictions at the hands of a hostile mankind and a potential for rescue through some undefined spiritual transcendence. Due to the constant interference of some unnamed evil, however, this divine state is never likely to be attained. Also featuring are those even more mystifying unnamed beings: 'The lonely one', 'The stranger', 'A dead one', 'A sick one', or even 'The boy' and 'The Grandson'. In the poem 'Helian', for example, several of these figures loom up and then fade. 'At vespers the stranger is lost in black November destruction…', 'Softly rolls the yellow moon above the young man's fever sheets…'.

'Helian' is a crucial poem in Trakl's development from memorable curiosity to major European poet, a poem in which he unleashes a less histrionic, more poetically controlled and intricate imagery, leaving behind some of the overly romantic pastoral verbiage or morbidly overblown, decadent images which tend to hamper some of the earlier experiments. The poem 'Helian' is an epic of derangement, a distillation of personal and communal suffering, the descent into an abyss of degraded innocence and eventual ascension from human chaos and bodily destruction through divine resurrection. Rilke wrote of 'Helian': 'It is built on its pauses, a few satisfactions about the limited wordless: so stand the lines. Like fences in a flat land beyond which extends the unfenced in a vastness which remains unpossessed.'

'Helian' introduces many of the themes and images which would occur repeatedly throughout Trakl's mature phase, a fact which has prompted many to ask whether individual poems are not in fact just one long work. The visionary potency of Trakl's language can obscure its limited range when compared to the work of other major European poets like Rilke or Baudelaire for example, and the brazen recycling of images coupled with an almost neurotic repetition has lead some critics to label his poetry kitsch or even demented nonsense, the mere babbling overflow of a schizoid personality. Such narrow views can, however, often be traced to nothing more complex than writerly envy, impatience with defining the enigmatic qualities of the poetry, or a tedious compulsion to say the opposite of the majority view. The fact is that Trakl's poetry comes from a profound inwardness which always chooses the vertical over the horizontal. It mines the same seam but will not give up that seam until all hope is lost and the world crashes in. Trakl, in order to survive, keeps digging down into that seam as long as there is something to be mined and until he finally runs out of air.

One of the most insistent images in Trakl's poetry is that of the 'sister'. The question of incest between Georg and his sister has never been resolved. What is more important is the repeated appearances of the sister figure in his poems, either as a real person ('In the next room, the sister is playing a Schubert sonata' from 'Wayfaring') or as a spectre ('The sister again appears in someone's evil dreams' from 'Psalm'). Perhaps fittingly she also appears in Trakl's final poem 'Grodek': 'The sister's shadow sways through the grove, to greet the ghosts of the heroes, the bleeding heads...'. The guilt of incest whether consummated or unconsummated is probably the greatest burden on Trakl's fragile psyche. In the early poem 'Dream of Evil', the incestuous relationship is made plain: 'Brother and sister spy on each other, trembling in the park...'. It is the flagship of his suffering around which a flotilla of other smaller craft crowd. The sister symbolises temptation, sin, childhood nostalgia, lost innocence. She is the shadow who never dies, the haunting presence, a being whom Trakl seems to be endowing with a reality more deserving of life than his own. As he fades out in decline, the sister endures since she is the spiritual entity standing for transcendence beyond the 'stony silence' of the material world. Like many other characters who appear in Trakl's poems, she is elusive and impossible to definitively interpret.

The interplay of colour, animal and human forms in metamorphosis, landscapes relating to particular moods and also those uncanny moments of spectral drama in the poems, bristling with derangement, seize their readers and force them to confront this alternative reality, or as Rilke puts it 'experience such spectacles and perceptions as though pressed, an exile, against a pane of glass...'

After the concentrated visionary force of 'Helian' there is a steady intensification of Trakl's despair and a corresponding tightening of the poems. Trakl returned obsessively to certain works, making alterations and honing them, even years later. In the last year and a half or so Trakl's poetry developed from the early strophic forms to a more hymnic style which clearly owes much to the growing influence of Hölderlin. Earlier Trakl had borrowed heavily from Rimbaud. In 'De Profundis' for example the repeated lines which begin 'There is... ' etc are lifted

straight out of Rimbaud's 'Childhood' from 'Illumina-
tions'. 'Rimbaud's line 'There is a pothole with a nest of
white animals' seems uncannily close to 'There is a room
which they have whitewashed with milk...' from 'Psalm'.
In fact the whole tone and imagery from these Rimbaud
poems courses through Trakl's work of this period. Even
'The little dead girl, behind the rose-bushes' in Part II of
'Childhood' seems to reappear in 'De Profundis' as the
orphan whose 'sweet remains' are found by shepherds
'decayed in the thornbush'. But Trakl only borrows the
Rimbaud style as a setting for his own very personal crea-
tions and despite the obvious comparisons the Trakl poem
secures its autonomy and uniqueness due to that innate
lack of pretence and contrivance with which his fugitive
dream language is imbued.

As he matured poetically, Trakl turned his back on the
formal rhyme which marks his earlier work and favoured
the use of free verse. This presumably gave him the free-
dom, flexibility and opportunity to deliver the pared-
down but formidable images he required to express him-
self in as uncompromising a way as possible. As his mor-
tal fears increased the later poems reflect a sense of
unrelieved brooding on destruction, both personal and
abstract as well as the terrifying prospect of the self being
finally overwhelmed. A poem like 'In the East' sends an
ominous veiled warning: 'Wild wolves have broken
through the gate'; but in one of the final poems, 'Lament',
he is much more explicit: 'The dark eagles night and death
nightlong sweep around this head...' In the same poem
the image of man's fall is rendered with unyielding fury:
'Eternity's icy wave would devour man's golden image,
against terrible reefs his purple frame is smashed.' Such
imagery seems to pre-empt the fate of mankind in the
murderous war to follow. Now, as a medical orderly
caught up in the shambles of the Galician campaign, all
those fears which had menaced him for so long took on a
terrible reality. This was the cataclysm he and mankind
had been heading towards, that which his acutely sensi-
tive psyche had glimpsed or more likely whose as yet

obscure bulk he had felt pressing from the future, just as later Kafka would the Holocaust, but which neither had been able to picture in its most unimaginable reality. The force and implication behind such a prophecy came through clear enough but the nature of the event itself remained in shadow.

Yet before this late stage Trakl was already expressing in notes and letters to Ficker the growing fear that he was about to lose himself completely to madness. 'Tell me that I must still have the strength to live and do what is true. Tell me that I am not insane. A stony darkness has broken in...' Even at this late hour Trakl still hopes for transcendence; despite the wearing down of his defences and the grim certainty that 'all roads lead to black putrefaction', in the last line of 'Grodek' he points perhaps to a possible future beyond earthly pain: 'Today a monstrous agony feeds the hot flame of the spirit, the unborn grandson.' And even following the frenzy of apocalyptic images in 'To the Silenced', he again closes soberly predicting the possibility of absolution. 'But in dark caves a mankind more silent bleeds, from hard metals forms the redeeming head'. In fact such solemn pronouncements appear to occur with greater frequency in poems which harbour monstrous visions of mankind's corruption and collapse. Flickering with insanity, lines like 'Oh the gruesome laughter of gold' or 'Whore who bears a child in icy convulsions' are the negative, destructive, 'convulsive' dark forces of reality which are countered at the end by the all-or-nothing charge from the white knight of redemption.

The fact that nothing follows this last declaration not only exacerbates its poignancy as the close of the poem but also allows nothing more to come from the destructive side. One is left with a profound silence resonating with unresolved implication, a sense of awe tempered by confusion. Although Trakl falls, he may yet be redeemed in that longed-for higher realm where he shall finally do penance for his 'melancholy crimes'.

Trakl's last poems, 'Klage' and 'Grodek',
witten on the reverse of the 'Testaments Brief', Trakl's final short
letter to Ficker from the military hospital in Krakow, 27 October, 1914.

Just before boarding the train for Galicia, the fledgling medical orderly handed a note to Ficker. As Trakl clambered aboard, Ficker read: 'Feelings in moments of death-like existence: all human beings are worthy of love. Awakening you sense the world's bitterness, in which resides all unresolved guilt; your poem an imperfect atonement.' The train pulled out. Trakl was drawn into the abyss of war and never returned.

PART III – FURTHER READING

Secondary works on Trakl of further interest are:

Sharpe, Francis Michael, *The Poet's Madness: A Reading of Georg Trakl* (Cornell University Press, 1981);

Detsch, Richard, *Georg Trakl's Poetry: Towards a Union of Opposites* (Penn State University Press, 1983);

Kurrik, Maire Jaanus, *Georg Trakl* (Columbia Essays on Modern Writers, 1972);

Lindenberger, Herbert, *Georg Trakl* (Twayne Publishers Inc., 1971);

Weichselbaum, Hans, *Georg Trakl – Eine Biographie mit Bildern, Texten und Dokumenten* (Otto Müller Verlag, Salzburg, 1994)*

* For those with some knowledge of German, the last book cited above is indispensable. A number of Trakl studies exist in his native language, of which this pictorial biography is the most comprehensive and accessible. It makes available an extensive picture and document archive, much of which has never been published before. At present, no biography or substantial account of Trakl's life and work currently exists in English at all. Most of the books listed above are out of print, but copies can be tracked down through internet bookdealers. A new and updated collected edition of Trakl's works in German is now in preparation.

TO THE SILENCED
SELECTED POEMS

DAS GRAUEN

Ich sah mich durch verlass'ne Zimmer gehn.
— Die Sterne tanzten irr auf blauem Grunde,
Und auf den Feldern heulten laut die Hunde,
Und in den Wipfeln wühlte wild der Föhn.

Doch plötzlich: Stille! Dumpfe Fieberglut
Läßt giftige Blumen blühn aus meinem Munde,
Aus dem Geäst fällt wie aus einer Wunde
Blaß schimmernd Tau, und fällt, und fällt wie Blut.

Aus eines Spiegels trügerischer Leere
Hebt langsam sich, und wie ins Ungefähre
Aus Graun und Finsternis ein Antlitz: Kain!

Sehr leise rauscht die samtene Portiere,
Durchs Fenster schaut der Mond gleichwie ins Leere,
Da bin mit meinem Mörder ich allein.

THE HORROR

I saw myself passing through abandoned rooms.
– The stars danced demented on a blue background
And lonely howled the dogs in the fields,
Madly heaved the wind in the tops of trees.

But suddenly: stillness! A dull fever glow
Commands venomous flowers to bloom from my mouth,
And from the branches dew falls as from a wound
Pale, shimmering and falls, and falls like blood.

Out of the treacherous vacancy of a mirror
A face rises slowly and imprecisely
Out of horror and darkness: Cain!

So softly whispers the velvet curtain,
Through the window the moon gazes out
As into emptiness,
There I am alone with my murderer.

ST. PETERS-FRIEDHOF

Ringsum ist Felseneinsamkeit.
Des Todes bleiche Blumen schauern
Auf Gräbern, die im Dunkel trauern –
Doch diese Trauer hat kein Leid.

Der Himmel lächelt still herab
In diesen traumverschlossenen Garten,
Wo stille Pilger seiner warten.
Es wacht das Kreuz auf jedem Grab.

Die Kirche ragt wie ein Gebet
Vor einem Bilde ewiger Gnaden,
Manch Licht brennt unter den Arkaden,
Das stumm für arme Seelen fleht —

Indes die Bäume blüh'n zur Nacht,
Daß sich des Todes Antlitz hülle
In ihrer Schönheit schimmernde Fülle,
Die Tote tiefer träumen macht.

ST PETER'S CHURCHYARD

Rock loneliness is all around.
The pale death flowers shudder
On graves, which in darkness mourn –
Yet this mourning knows no pain.

Calmly heaven smiles down
Into this dream-enclosed garden,
Where peaceful pilgrims await it.
Over every grave the cross keeps watch.

The church towers up as to prayer
Before an image of grace eternal,
Many a candle burns beneath the arches
And mutely petitions holy souls –

Meanwhile the trees blossom by night,
That death would his countenance conceal
Within their beauty's shimmering fullness,
Which makes the dead dream deeper still.

WINTERDÄMMERUNG
An Max von Esterle

Schwarze Himmel von Metall.
Kreuz in roten Stürmen wehen
Abends hungertolle Krähen
Über Parken gram und fahl.

Im Gewölk erfriert ein Strahl;
Und vor Satans Flüchen drehen
Jene sich im Kreis und gehen
Nieder siebenfach an Zahl.

In Verfaultem süß und schal
Lautlos ihre Schnäbel mähen.
Häuser dräu'n aus stummen Nähen;
Helle im Theatersaal.

Kirchen, Brücken und Spital
Grauenvoll im Zwielicht stehen.
Blutbefleckte Linnen blähen
Segel sich auf dem Kanal.

WINTER DUSK

To Max von Esterle

Black skies of metal.
Crossing in red storms at dusk
Hunger-crazed crows drift
Over the park pale and mournful.

In cloud a beam is deathly frozen;
And by Satan's curse they wheel
Full circle and go down
Seven in number.

In putrefaction, sweet and stale
Soundless their beaks are carving.
From mute closeness dwellings threaten;
Bright light in the auditorium.

Church, bridge and hospital
Stand terrible in the twilight
Blood-spattered linen billows out
Sails on the canal.

ROMANZE ZUR NACHT

Einsamer unterm Sternenzelt
Geht durch die stille Mitternacht.
Der Knab aus Träumen wirr erwacht,
Sein Antlitz grau im Mond verfällt.

Die Närrin weint mit offnem Haar
Am Fenster, das vergittert starrt.
Im Teich vorbei auf süßer Fahrt
Ziehn Liebende sehr wunderbar.

Der Mörder lächelt bleich im Wein,
Den Kranken Todesgrauen packt.
Die Nonne betet wund und nackt
Vor des Heilands Kreuzespein.

Die Mutter leis im Schlafe singt.
Sehr friedlich schaut zur Nacht das Kind
Mit Augen, die ganz wahrhaft sind.
Im Hurenhaus Gelächter klingt.

Beim Talglicht drunt' im Kellerloch
Der Tote malt mit weißer Hand
Ein grinsend Schweigen an die Wand.
Der Schläfer flüstert immer noch.

ROMANCE TO NIGHT

Beneath a tent of stars the lonely one
Moves through the stillness of midnight.
The boy wakes, reeling from his dreams,
His grey face wasting into the moon.

At the window rigid with bars
Weeps the idiot woman with gaping hair.
The lovers drift by on the pond
Their sweet journey truly a miracle.

The murderer smiles waxen into the wine,
Death's horror devours the afflicted.
A nun prays naked and wounded
Before the crucified saviour's fearful anguish.

A mother sings softly in sleep.
With eyes wholly pure, truly at peace
A child gazes into the night.
Laughter breaks out from whorehouse.

By candlelight, with whitened hand
The dead down in the cellar hole
Paint smirking silence upon the walls.
But still the sleeper continues to whisper.

DIE RATTEN

Im Hof scheint weiß der herbstliche Mond.
Vom Dachrand fallen phantastische Schatten.
Ein Schweigen in leeren Fenstern wohnt;
Da tauchen leise herauf die Ratten

Und huschen pfeifend hier und dort
Und ein gräulicher Dunsthauch wittert
Ihnen nach aus dem Abort,
Den geisterhaft der Mondschein durchzittert.

Und sie keifen vor Gier wie toll
Und erfüllen Haus und Scheunen,
Die von Korn und Früchten voll.
Eisige Winde im Dunkel greinen.

THE RATS

In the courtyard the autumn moon shines white.
From the roof's edge fantastic shadows fall.
A silence dwells in empty windows;
Where softly the rats rise up

And whistling scurry here and there.
A greyish dust-haze breathes
After them from the latrine, through which
The ghostly moonlight shivers.

And insatiably they squabble, as if insane
Crowding into house and barns,
Filled with fruit and grain.
In the darkness icy winds complain.

TRAUM DES BÖSEN

Verhallend eines Sterbeglöckchens Klänge –
Ein Liebender erwacht in schwarzen Zimmern
Die Wang' an Sternen, die im Fenster flimmern.
Am Strome blitzen Segel, Masten, Stränge.

Ein Mönch, ein schwangres Weib dort im Gedränge.
Gitarren klimpern, rote Kittel schimmern.
Kastanien schwül in goldnem Glanz verkümmern;
Schwarz ragt der Kirchen trauriges Gepränge.

Aus bleichen Masken schaut der Geist des Bösen.
Ein Platz verdämmert grauenvoll und düster;
Am Abend regt auf Inseln sich Geflüster.

Des Vogelfluges wirre Zeichen lesen
Aussätzige, die zur Nacht vielleicht verwesen.
Im Park erblicken zitternd sich Geschwister.

DREAM OF EVIL

A gong's sound, dying out –
A lover wakes in black chambers
Cheek to stars, that flicker at the window.
On the river, rope, mast and sail blaze.

A monk, a pregnant woman in the crowd.
Guitars that strum, the shimmer of scarlet frocks.
Sultry, in golden gleams the chestnuts wither away;
Black looms the churches' dismal panoply.

From pale masks peers the spirit of evil.
A square darkens morbid and terrible;
Whispers well up on the islands at nightfall.

Lepers who may rot away at night
Read confused omens from the bird flight.
Brother and sister spy on each other
Trembling in the park.

PSALM
Karl Kraus zugeeignet

Es ist ein Licht, das der Wind ausgelöscht hat.
Es ist ein Heidekrug, den am Nachmittag ein Betrunkener
    verläßt.
Es ist ein Weinberg, verbrannt und schwarz mit
    Löchern voll von Spinnen.
Es ist ein Raum, den sie mit Milch getüncht haben.
Der Wahnsinnige ist gestorben. Es ist eine Insel der
    Südsee,
Den Sonnengott zu empfangen. Man rührt die Trommeln.
Die Männer führen kriegerische Tänze auf.
Die Frauen wiegen die Hüften in Schlinggewächsen und
    Feuerblumen,
Wenn das Meer singt. O unser verlorenes Paradies.

Die Nymphen haben die goldenen Wälder verlassen.
Man begräbt den Fremden. Dann hebt ein
    Flimmerregen an.
Der Sohn des Pan erscheint in Gestalt eines Erdarbeiters,
Der den Mittag am glühenden Asphalt verschläft.
Es sind kleine Mädchen in einem Hof in Kleidchen
    voll herzzerreissender Armut!
Es sind Zimmer, erfüllt von Akkorden und Sonaten.
Es sind Schatten, die sich vor einem erblindeten
    Spiegel umarmen.
An den Fenstern des Spitals wärmen sich Genesende.
Ein weisser Dampfer am Kanal trägt blutige Seuchen herauf.

Die fremde Schwester erscheint wieder in jemands bösen
    Träumen.
Ruhend im Haselgebüsch spielt sie mit seinen Sternen.
Der Student, vielleicht ein Doppelgänger, schaut ihr lange
    vom Fenster nach.

PSALM
For Karl Kraus

There is a light which the wind has extinguished.
There is an inn on the heath, which a drunk abandons
     in the afternoon.
There is a vineyard, black and burnt with holes full of spiders.
There is a room, which they have whitewashed with milk.
The madman has perished. There is an island of the
     South Sea,
To receive the sun god. Drums are beaten.
The men lead dances of war.
The women hipsway in fireflowers and creepers,
When the sea sings. O our lost paradise.

The nymphs have left the golden woods.
The stranger is buried. Then a shimmering rain arises.
The son of Pan appears as an earthworker,
Who sleeps through noon against the glowing asphalt.
There are little girls in a courtyard in tiny frocks
     full of heart-rending want!
There are rooms filled with accords and sonatas.
There are shadows which embrace before a mirror
     gone blind.
At the windows of hospitals convalescents warm
     themselves.
Up the canal a white steamer carries the bloody epidemic.

The sister again appears in someone's evil dreams.
Resting in the hazel bush she plays with his stars.
The student, perhaps a double, follows her from the
     window for a long time.

Hinter ihm steht sein toter Bruder, oder er geht die Alte
Wendeltreppe herab.
Im Dunkel brauner Kastanien verblasst die Gestalt des
jungen Novizen.
Der Garten ist im Abend. Im Kreuzgang flattern die
Fledermäuse umher.
Die Kinder des Hausmeisters hören zu spielen auf und
suchen das Gold des Himmels.
Endakkorde eines Quartetts. Die kleine Blinde läuft
zitternd durch die Allee,
Und später tastet ihr Schatten an kalten Mauern hin,
umgeben von Märchen und heiligen Legenden.

Es ist ein leeres Boot, das am Abend den schwarzen
Kanal heruntertreibt.
In der Düsternis des alten Asyls verfallen menschliche
Ruinen.
Die toten Waisen liegen an der Gartenmauer.
Aus grauen Zimmern treten Engel mit kotgefleckten
Flügeln.
Würmer tropfen von ihren vergilbten Lidern.
Der Platz vor der Kirche ist finster und schweigsam,
wie in den Tagen der Kindheit.
Auf silbernen Sohlen gleiten frühere Leben vorbei
Und die Schatten der Verdammten steigen zu den
seufzenden Wassern nieder.
In seinem Grab spielt der weisse Magier mit seinen
Schlangen.

Schweigsam über der Schädelstätte öffnen sich Gottes
goldene Augen.

Behind him stands his dead brother, or else he descends
     the old spiral staircase.
In darkness, brown chestnut trees fade the figure
     of the young novice.
The garden is in evening. Bats flutter about the cloister.
The caretaker's children surrender play and seek the gold
     of heaven.
Final chord of a quartet. The little blind girl runs trembling
     down the avenue.
And later her shadow feels its way along cold walls,
     surrounded by fairytales and holy legends.

There is an empty boat, which drifts down the black canal
     at evening.
In the gloom of the old asylum human ruins decay.
The dead orphans lie by the garden wall.
From grey rooms step angels with filth-spattered wings.
Worms drip from their yellowed lids.
The square before the church is dark and silent,
     as in the days of childhood.
On silver soles earlier lives glide by
And the shadows of the damned decline towards
     the sighing waters.
In his grave the white magician plays with his serpents.

Silently above the place of skulls God's golden eyes
     are opening.

TRÜBSINN

Weltunglück geistert durch den Nachmittag.
Baracken fliehn durch Gärtchen braun und wüst.
Lichtschnuppen gaukeln um verbrannten Mist,
Zwei Schläfer schwanken heimwärts, grau und vag.

Auf der verdorrten Wiese läuft ein Kind
Und spielt mit seinen Augen schwarz und glatt.
Das Gold tropft von den Büschen trüb und matt.
Ein alter Mann dreht traurig sich im Wind.

Am Abend wieder über meinem Haupt
Saturn lenkt stumm ein elendes Geschick.
Ein Baum, ein Hund tritt hinter sich zurück
Und schwarz schwankt Gottes Himmel und entlaubt.

Ein Fischlein gleitet schnell hinab den Bach;
Und leise rührt des toten Freundes Hand
Und glättet liebend Stirne und Gewand.
Ein Licht ruft Schatten in den Zimmern wach.

DEJECTION

Through afternoon the spectre of world calamity.
Huts flee through little gardens brown and forlorn.
Guttering light hovers around burnt manure,
Two sleepers sway homewards, grey and obscure.

On the withered grass a child runs
And plays with his eyes black and smooth.
Gold drips from bushes dreary and bleak.
An old man turns sadly in the wind.

At nightfall once more above my head
Saturn mutely steers a wretched fate.
A tree, a dog steps back behind itself
And black reels God's heaven and defoliates.

A little fish glides quickly down the stream;
And softly stirs the dead friend's hand
And lovingly smoothes brow and garment.
A light bids shadows in the rooms awake.

DE PROFUNDIS

Es ist ein Stoppelfeld, in das ein schwarzer Regen fällt.
Es ist ein brauner Baum, der einsam dasteht.
Es ist ein Zischelwind, der leere Hütten umkreist –
Wie traurig dieser Abend.

Am Weiler vorbei
Sammelt die sanfte Waise noch spärliche Ähren ein.
Ihre Augen weiden rund und goldig in der Dämmerung
Und ihr Schoß harrt des himmlischen Bräutigams.

Bei der Heimkehr
Fanden die Hirten den süßen Leib
Verwest im Dornenbusch.

Ein Schatten bin ich ferne finsteren Dörfern.
Gottes Schweigen
Trank ich aus dem Brunnen des Hains.

Auf meine Stirne tritt kaltes Metall.
Spinnen suchen mein Herz.
Es ist ein Licht, das in meinem Mund erlöscht.

Nachts fand ich mich auf einer Heide,
Starrend von Unrat und Staub der Sterne.
Im Haselgebüsch
Klangen wieder kristallne Engel.

DE PROFUNDIS

There is a stubble field where a black rain falls.
There is a brown tree here, which stands alone.
There is a hissing wind that wreathes the empty huts –
How sorrowful this evening.

Beyond the hamlet
The gentle orphan still gathers in the meagre grain.
Round and golden her eyes graze in the twilight
And her womb awaits the heavenly bridegroom.

Returning home
Shepherds found the sweet remains
Decayed in the thorn bush.

A shadow I am far from darkened villages.
God's silence
I drank from the spring in the grove.

Onto my brow cold metal steps.
Spiders seek my heart.
There is a light that dies in my mouth.

At night I found myself upon a heath,
Thick with filth and stardust.
In the hazel copse
Crystal angels have chimed again.

TROMPETEN

Unter verschnittenen Weiden, wo braune Kinder spielen
Und Blätter treiben, tönen Trompeten. Ein
    Kirchhofschauer.
Fahnen von Scharlach stürzen durch des Ahorns Trauer,
Reiter entlang an Roggenfeldern, leeren Mühlen.

Oder Hirten singen nachts und Hirsche treten
In den Kreis ihrer Feuer, des Hains uralte Trauer,
Tanzende heben sich von einer schwarzen Mauer;
Fahnen von Scharlach, Lachen, Wahnsinn, Trompeten.

MENSCHHEIT

Menschheit vor Feuerschlünden aufgestellt,
Ein Trommelwirbel, dunkler Krieger Stirnen,
Schritte durch Blutnebel; schwarzes Eisen schellt;
Verzweiflung, Nacht in traurigen Gehirnen:
Hier Evas Schatten, Jagd und rotes Geld.
Gewölk, das Licht durchbricht, das Abendmahl.
Es wohnt in Brot und Wein ein sanftes Schweigen.
Und jene sind versammelt zwölf an Zahl.
Nachts schrein im Schlaf sie unter Ölbaumzweigen;
Sankt Thomas taucht die Hand ins Wundenmal.

TRUMPETS

Beneath trimmed willows, where brown children play
And leaves scatter, the trumpets sound.
    Graveyard shudder.
Banners of scarlet plunge through the maple's grief
Riders along rye fields, abandoned mills.

Or shepherds sing at night and stags step
Into the circle of their fire, the grove's age old sorrow,
Dancers rise up from a black wall;
Banners of scarlet, laughter, madness, trumpets.

MANKIND

Mankind before the chosen fire chasms,
Dark brows of warriors, a roll of drums,
Footsteps in blood fog; black irons sound;
Despair, night spent in the downcast mind:
Eve's shadow comes, red coins and the hunt.
Cloud where light breaks through,
The last supper.
A gentle silence dwells in bread and wine.
And those twelve in number there;
Nightly beneath olive trees they cry out in sleep;
Saint Thomas dips his hand into the wound.

DREI BLICKE IN EINEN OPAL

An Erhard Buschbeck

1.

Blick in Opal: ein Dorf umkränzt von dürrem Wein,
Der Stille grauer Wolken, gelber Felsenhügel
Und abendlicher Quellen Kühle: Zwillingsspiegel
Umrahmt von Schatten und von schleimigem Gestein.

Des Herbstes Weg und Kreuze gehn in Abend ein,
Singende Pilger und die blutbefleckten Linnen.
Des Einsamen Gestalt kehrt also sich nach innen
Und geht, ein bleicher Engel, durch den leeren Hain.

Aus Schwarzem bläst der Föhn. Mit Satyrn im Verein
Sind schlanke Weiblein; Mönche der Wollust bleiche
          Priester,
Ihr Wahnsinn schmückt mit Lilien sich schön und düster
Und hebt die Hände auf zu Gottes goldenem Schrein.

2.

Der ihn befeuchtet, rosig hängt ein Tropfen Tau
Im Rosmarin: hinfließt ein Hauch von Grabgerüchen,
Spitälern, wirr erfüllt von Fieberschrein und Flüchen.
Gebein steigt aus dem Erbbegräbnis morsch und grau.

In blauem Schleim und Schleiern tanzt des Greisen Frau,
Das schmutzstarrende Haar erfüllt von schwarzen Tränen,
Die Knaben träumen wirr in dürren Weidensträhnen
Und ihre Stirnen sind von Aussatz kahl und rauh.

Durchs Bogenfenster sinkt der Abend lind und lau.
Ein Heiliger tritt aus seinen schwarzen Wundenmalen.
Die Purpurschnecken kriechen aus zerbrochenen Schalen
Und speien Blut in Dorngewinde starr und grau.

THREE GLANCES INTO AN OPAL
To Erhard Buschbeck

1.

Glance into an opal: a village wreathed in withered vines,
Stillness of grey clouds, yellow rocky mounds
And coolness of the evening spring: twin mirrors
Framed by shadows and slimy stones.

Autumn paths and crosses settle into evening,
Singing pilgrims and blood-stained linen.
Thus the figure of the solitary turns inward
And travels, a pale angel through the deserted grove.

From blackness blows the föhn. With satyrs
The slender young women unite; monks, pale lustful
        priests,
Their madness embellished with dark and lovely lilies
Raise their hands to the golden shrine of God.

2.

A dew drop hangs reddish, its moisture
For the Rosemary: a stench of graves leaks away.
Hospitals, swollen with the madness of fever moans and curses.
From the grey and mouldered family vault a skeleton ascends.

In blue haze and slime the old man's wife dances,
Her filth-stiffened hair brimming with black tears.
Boys dream wildly amongst barren willow fronds
Their brows bare and raw with leprosy.

Through the arched window evening settles balmy and mild.
A saint steps from his wounds' black scars.
Crimson snails crawl from broken shells
And spurt blood into stiffened grey thorn snarls.

3.

Die Blinden streuen in eiternde Wunden Weiherauch.
Rorgoldene Gewänder; Fackeln; Psalmensingen;
Und Mädchen, die wie Gift den Leib des Herrn
    umschlingen.
Gestalten schreiten wächsernstarr durch Glut und Rauch.

Aussätziger mitternächtigen Tanz führt an ein Gauch
Dürrknöchern. Garten wunderlicher Abenteuer;
Verzerrtes; Blumenfratzen, Lachen; Ungeheuer
Und rollendes Gestirn im schwarzen Dornenstrauch.

O Armut, Bettelsuppe, Brot und süßer Lauch;
Des Lebens Träumerei in Hütten vor den Wäldern.
Grau härtet sich der Himmel über gelben Feldern
Und eine Abendglocke singt nach altem Brauch.

3.

The blind spread incense into festering wounds.
Red golden gowns; torchlight, the singing of psalms;
And girls who embrace the Lord's body like poison.
Figures stride wax-stiffened through embers and smoke.

A dry-boned fool leads the lepers in a midnight dance.
Gardens of outlandish adventure;
Distortions; grotesque flower faces, laughter; ogres,
And rolling stars in black thorny briars.

O poverty, beggars' broth, bread and sweet leek;
Life's daydream in a hut on the forest edge.
Grey hardens the sky above the yellow fields
And as is the custom, the evening bells sing out.

ZU ABEND MEIN HERZ

Am Abend hört man den Schrei der Fledermäuse,
Zwei Rappen springen auf der Wiese,
Der rote Ahorn rauscht.
Dem Wanderer erscheint die kleine Schenke am Weg.
Herrlich schmecken junger Wein und Nüsse,
Herrlich: betrunken zu taumeln in dämmernden Wald.
Durch schwarzes Geäst tönen schmerzliche Glokken,
Auf das Gesicht tropft Tau.

NÄHE DES TODES

O der Abend, der in die finsteren Dörfer der Kindheit geht.
Der Weiher unter den Weiden
Füllt sich mit den verpesteten Seufzern der Schwermut.

O der Wald, der leise die braunen Augen senkt,
Da aus des Einsamen knöchernen Händen
Der Purpur seiner verzückten Tage hinsinkt.

O die Nähe des Todes. Laß uns beten.
In dieser Nacht lösen auf lauen Kissen
Vergilbt von Weihrauch sich der Liebenden schmächtige
    Glieder.

MY HEART TOWARDS EVENING

At evening you hear the shriek of bats,
Two black horses leap in the meadow,
Rustling of the red maple.
To the wayfarer on the road the modest inn appears.
Heavenly to taste the nuts and new wine,
Heavenly: to lurch drunkenly through the dusking wood.
From black branches grief stricken bells are sounding,
Dew drips on your face.

NEARNESS OF DEATH

O the evening, that enters the dark hamlets
Of childhood.
The pond beneath the willows
Fills with the blighted sighs of melancholy.

O the forest which softly lowers brown eyes,
As from the lonely one's bony hands
The crimson of his rapturous days sinks down.

O the nearness of death. Let us pray.
In this night the frail limbs of lovers
Yellowed with incense on warm cushions break free.

AMEN

Verwestes gleitend durch die morsche Stube;
Schatten an gelben Tapeten; in dunklen Spiegeln wölbt
Sich unserer Hände elfenbeinerne Traurigkeit.

Braune Perlen rinnen durch die erstorbenen Finger.
In der Stille
Tun sich eines Engels blaue Mohnaugen auf.

Blau ist auch der Abend;
Die Stunde unseres Absterbens, Azraels Schatten,
Der ein braunes Gärtchen verdunkelt.

AMEN

Corruption gliding through the mouldered room;
Shadows on yellow wallpaper; in dark mirrors
The ivory sorrow of our hands is arched.

Brown beads trickle through perished fingers.
In the stillness
An angel's opiate eyes of blue.

The evening also is blue;
The hour of our demise, Azrael's shadow,
Darkening a little brown garden.

HELIAN

I

In den einsamen Stunden des Geistes
Ist es schön, in der Sonne zu gehn
An den gelben Mauern des Sommers hin.
Leise klingen die Schritte im Gras; doch immer schläft
Der Sohn des Pan im grauen Marmor.

Abends auf der Terrasse betranken wir uns mit braunem
    Wein.
Rötlich glüht der Pfirsich im Laub;
Sanfte Sonate, frohes Lachen.

Schön ist die Stille der Nacht.
Auf dunklem Plan
Begegnen wir uns mit Hirten und weißen Sternen.

Wenn es Herbst geworden ist,
Zeigt sich nüchterne Klarheit im Hain.
Besänftigte wandeln wir an roten Mauern hin
Und die runden Augen folgen dem Flug der Vögel.
Am Abend sinkt das weiße Wasser in Graburnen.

In kahlen Gezweigen feiert der Himmel.
In reinen Händen trägt der Landmann Brot und Wein
Und friedlich reifen die Früchte in sonniger Kammer.

O wie ernst ist das Antlitz der teuren Toten.
Doch die Seele erfreut gerechtes Anschaun.

HELIAN

I

In the solitary hours of the spirit
Beautiful it is to walk in the sun,
By the yellow walls of summer.
Quietly our footsteps ring in the grass; but always
The son of Pan sleeps in the grey marble.

Evenings on the terrace we were drunk on brown wine.
Reddish glows the peach in the leaves;
Soft sonata, cheerful laughter.

Beautiful is the stillness of night.
On the dark plain
We meet with shepherds and white stars.

When Autumn comes
A sober clarity enters the grove.
Soothed, we wander beside red walls
And round eyes follow the flight of birds.
At evening white water sinks down in the funeral urns.

In bare branches heaven rejoices.
In pure hands the countryman carries bread and wine
And peacefully ripens the fruit in the sunny pantry.

O how earnest is the countenance of the dear deceased.
Yet the soul delights in righteous contemplation.

II

Gewaltig ist das Schweigen des verwüsteten Gartens,
Da der junge Novize die Stirne mit braunem Laub bekränzt,
Sein Odem eisiges Gold trinkt.

Die Hände rühren das Alter bläulicher Wasser
Oder in kalter Nacht die weißen Wangen der Schwestern.

Leise und harmonisch ist ein Gang an freundlichen
        Zimmern hin,
Wo Einsamkeit ist und das Rauschen des Ahorns,
Wo vielleicht noch die Drossel singt.

Schön ist der Mensch und erscheinend im Dunkel,
Wenn er staunend Arme und Beine bewegt,
Und in purpurnen Höhlen stille die Augen rollen.

Zur Vesper verliert sich der Fremdling in schwarzer
        Novemberzerstörung,
Unter morschem Geäst, an Mauern voll Aussatz hin,
Wo vordem der heilige Bruder gegangen,
Versunken in das sanfte Saitenspiel seines Wahnsinns.

O wie einsam endet der Abendwind.
Ersterbend neigt sich das Haupt im Dunkel des Ölbaums.

II

Immense is the silence of the ruined garden
When the young novice wreathes his brow with brown leaves,
His breath drinks icy gold.

Hands stir the age of bluish waters
Or in cold night the white cheeks of the sisters.

Soft and harmonious is a walk past friendly rooms,
Where solitude is and the rustle of the maple,
Where perhaps the thrush still sings.

Beautiful is man and emerging in darkness,
When marvelling he moves his limbs,
And silently his eyes roll in crimson hollows.

At vespers the stranger is lost in black November
          destruction,
Beneath rotting boughs, by walls filled with leprosy,
Where the holy brother earlier walked,
Lost in the soft string play of his madness.

O how lonely dies the evening wind.
Failing, the head bows down in the olive tree darkness.

III

Erschütternd ist der Untergang des Geschlechts.
In dieser Stunde füllen sich die Augen des Schauenden
Mit dem Gold seiner Sterne.

Am Abend versinkt ein Glockenspiel, das nicht mehr tönt,
Verfallen die schwarzen Mauern am Platz,
Ruft der tote Soldat zum Gebet.

Ein bleicher Engel
Tritt der Sohn ins leere Haus seiner Väter.

Die Schwestern sind ferne zu weißen Greisen gegangen.
Nachts fand sie der Schläfer unter den Säulen im Hausflur,
Zurückgekehrt von traurigen Pilgerschaften.

O wie starrt von Kot und Würmern ihr Haar,
Da er darein mit silbernen Füßen steht,
Und jene verstorben aus kahlen Zimmern treten.

O ihr Psalmen in feurigen Mitternachtsregen,
Da die Knechte mit Nesseln die sanften Augen schlugen,
Die kindlichen Früchte des Holunders
Sich staunend neigen über ein leeres Grab.

Leise rollen vergilbte Monde
Über die Fieberlinnen des Jünglings,
Eh dem Schweigen des Winters folgt.

III

Shattering is the downfall of this race,
At this hour the eyes of the watcher
Fill with the gold of his stars.

At evening the dying bell, that chimes no more,
The decay of black walls on the square,
The dead soldier called to prayer.

A pale angel
The son steps into the empty house of his Fathers.

The sisters have gone far away to white old men,
At night the sleeper found them beneath the pillars
        in the hallway,
Returned from their mournful pilgrimages.

O how their hair stiffens with filth and worms,
As with silver feet he stands there,
And deceased, they step from bare rooms.

O you psalms in fiery midnight rains,
When with nettles the servants scourged the gentle eyes,
The childlike fruits of the elder
Incline astonished over an empty grave.

Softly rolls the yellowed moon
Above the young man's fever sheets,
Before the silence of winter comes.

IV

Ein erhabenes Schicksal sinnt den Kidron hinab,
Wo die Zeder, ein weiches Geschöpf,
Sich unter den blauen Brauen des Vaters entfaltet,
Über die Weide nachts ein Schäfer seine Herde führt.
Oder es sind Schreie im Schlaf,
Wenn ein eherner Engel im Hain den Menschen antritt,
Das Fleisch des Heiligen auf glühendem Rost hinschmilzt.

Um die Lehmhütten rankt purpurner Wein,
Tönende Bündel vergilbten Korns,
Das Summen der Bienen, der Flug des Kranichs.
Am Abend begegnen sich Auferstandene auf Felsenpfaden.

In schwarzen Wassern spiegeln sich Aussätzige;
Oder sie öffnen die kotbefleckten Gewänder
Weinend dem balsamischen Wind, der vom rosigen
      Hügel weht.

Schlanke Mägde tasten durch die Gassen der Nacht,
Ob sie den liebenden Hirten fänden.
Sonnabends tönt in den Hütten sanfter Gesang.

Lasset das Lied auch des Knaben gedenken,
Seines Wahnsinns, und weißer Brauen und seines
      Hingangs,
Des Verwesten, der bläulich die Augen aufschlägt.
O wie traurig ist dieses Wiedersehn.

An exalted destiny is pondered down past Kidron,
Where the cedar, a gentle creature,
Unfolds beneath the blue brow of the father,
A shepherd leads his flock over the meadow at night.
Or there are cries in sleep
When in the grove a brazen angel confronts man
The flesh of the saint melts on the glowing grill.

Round huts of clay the purple vines entwine,
Sheaves of yellowed corn resounding,
The hum of bees, the flight of cranes.
At evening on rocky paths the resurrected meet.

In black waters the lepers are mirrored
Or they part their filth-stained robes,
Weeping to the balsam wind that wafts down from the
        rosy hill.

Slender servant girls grope through the alleys of night,
To seek the loving shepherd.
On Saturdays gentle singing sounds in the huts.

May the song also remember the boy,
His madness, and white temples, his departing,
The decayed, who opens bluish his eyes.
O how wretched is this reunion.

V

Die Stufen des Wahnsinns in schwarzen Zimmern,
Die Schatten der Alten unter der offenen Tür,
Da Helians Seele sich im rosigen Spiegel beschaut
Und Schnee und Aussatz von seiner Stirne sinken.

An den Wänden sind die Sterne erloschen
Und die weißen Gestalten des Lichts.

Dem Teppich entsteigt Gebein der Gräber,
Das Schweigen verfallener Kreuze am Hügel,
Des Weihrauchs Süße im purpurnen Nachtwind.

0 ihr zerbrochenen Augen in schwarzen Mündern,
Da der Enkel in sanfter Umnachtung
Einsam dem dunkleren Ende nachsinnt,
Der stille Gott die blauen Lider über ihn senkt.

V

Steps of madness in black rooms,
Shadows of old men under the open door,
When Helian's soul regards itself in the rosy mirror
And from his brow snow and leprosy falls.

Along the walls the stars have died out
And the shapes of white light.

From carpets rise the bones of the graves,
On the hill the silence of crosses decayed,
Incense sweetness on the crimson night wind.

O you broken eyes in black mouths,
When the grandson in gentle derangement
Solitary, ponders the darker end,
The peaceful god lowers blue eyelids over him.

UNTERGANG

An Karl Borromäus Heinrich

Über den weißen Weiher
Sind die wilden Vögel fortgezogen.
Am Abend weht von unseren Sternen ein eisiger Wind.

Über unsere Gräber
Beugt sich die zerbrochene Stirne der Nacht.
Unter Eichen schaukeln wir auf einem silbernen Kahn.

Immer klingen die weißen Mauern der Stadt.
Unter Dornenbogen
O mein Bruder klimmen wir blinde Zeiger gen
        Mitternacht.

DECLINE

To Karl Borromäus Heinrich

Over the white pond,
The wild birds have journeyed on.
At evening an icy wind blows from our stars.

Over our graves
Leans the shattered brow of night.
Beneath oaks we rock in a silver boat.

Ever the white walls of the city ring out.
Beneath arches of thorn
O my brother, our blind hour-hands climb towards
        midnight.

AN DEN KNABEN ELIS

Elis, wenn die Amsel im schwarzen Wald ruft,
Dieses ist dein Untergang.
Deine Lippen trinken die Kühle des blauen Felsenquells.

Laß, wenn deine Stirne leise blutet
Uralte Legenden
Und dunkle Deutung des Vogelflugs.

Du aber gehst mit weichen Schritten in die Nacht,
Die voll purpurner Trauben hängt,
Und du regst die Arme schöner im Blau.

Ein Dornenbusch tönt,
Wo deine mondenen Augen sind.
O, wie lange bist, Elis, du verstorben.

Dein Leib ist eine Hyazinthe,
In die ein Mönch die wächsernen Finger taucht.
Eine schwarze Höhle ist unser Schweigen,

Daraus bisweilen ein sanftes Tier tritt
Und langsam die schweren Lider senkt.
Auf deine Schläfen tropft schwarzer Tau,

Das letzte Gold verfallener Sterne.

TO THE BOY ELIS

Elis, when the blackbird calls in the black wood,
This is your downfall.
Your lips drink in the coolness of the blue rock spring.

Leave be, when quietly your brow bleeds
Bygone legends
And the dark interpretation of bird flight.

But you walk with soft steps into the night,
Which is heavy with purple grapes,
And move your arms more beautifully in the blue.

A thorn bush sounds,
Where your moon eyes are.
O, how long, Elis, have you been dead.

Your body is a hyacinth,
Into which a monk dips his waxen fingers.
A black cavern is our silence,

From which at times a gentle animal steps
And slowly lowers heavy lids.
On your temples black dew drips,

The final gold of failed stars.

ELIS

I

Vollkommen ist die Stille dieses goldenen Tags.
Unter alten Eichen
Erscheinst du, Elis, ein Ruhender mit runden Augen.

Ihre Bläue spiegelt den Schlummer der Liebenden.
An deinem Mund
Verstummten ihre rosigen Seufzer.

Am Abend zog der Fischer die schweren Netze ein.
Ein guter Hirt
Führt seine Herde am Waldsaum hin.
O! wie gerecht sind, Elis, alle deine Tage.

Leise sinkt
An kahlen Mauern des Ölbaumes blaue Stille,
Erstirbt eines Greisen dunkler Gesang.

Ein goldener Kahn
Schaukelt, Elis, dein Herz am einsamen Himmel.

II

Ein sanftes Glockenspiel tönt in Elis' Brust
Am Abend,
Da sein Haupt ins schwarze Kissen sinkt.

Ein blaues Wild
Blutet leise im Dornengestrüpp.

Ein brauner Baum steht abgeschieden da;
Seine blauen Früchte fielen von ihm.

ELIS

Complete is the stillness of this golden day.
Under ancient oaks,
You appear, Elis, a restful one with round eyes.

Their blueness mirrors the slumber of lovers.
Upon your mouth
Their rosy sighs died out.

At evening the fisherman hauled in his heavy nets.
A good shepherd
Leads his flock by the forest edge.
Oh how righteous, Elis, are all your days.

Softly sinks
On stark walls the olive tree's blue stillness,
An old man's dark song died away.

A golden boat
Sways, Elis, your heart against a lonely sky.

II

In Elis' breast a gentle bell chime sounds
At evening,
When upon the black pillow his head sinks down.

A blue deer
Bleeds softly in the thorny thicket.

A brown tree stands secluded there,
Its blue fruits have fallen away.

Zeichen und Sterne
Versinken leise im Abendweiher.

Hinter dem Hügel ist es Winter geworden.

Blaue Tauben
Trinken nachts den eisigen Schweiß,
Der von Elis' kristallener Stirne rinnt.
Immer tönt
An schwarzen Mauern Gottes einsamer Wind.

Symbols and stars
Sink softly in the evening pond.

Behind the hill winter has come.

Blue doves
Nightly drink the icy sweat
That runs from Elis' crystal brow.
Forever
On black walls God's lonely wind resounds.

UNTERWEGS

Am Abend trugen sie den Fremden in die Totenkammer;
Ein Duft von Teer; das leise Rauschen roter Platanen;
Der dunkle Flug der Dohlen; am Platz zog eine
    Wache auf.
Die Sonne ist in schwarze Linnen gesunken; immer
    wieder kehrt dieser vergangene Abend.
Im Nebenzimmer spielt die Schwester eine Sonate von
    Schubert.
Sehr leise sinkt ihr Lächeln in den verfallenen Brunnen,
Der bläulich in der Dämmerung rauscht. O, wie alt ist
    unser Geschlecht.
Jemand flüstert drunten im Garten; jemand hat diesen
    schwarzen Himmel verlassen.
Auf der Kommode duften Äpfel. Großmutter zündet
    goldene Kerzen an.

O, wie mild ist der Herbst. Leise klingen unsere Schritte
    im alten Park
Unter hohen Bäumen. O, wie ernst ist das hyazinthene
    Antlitz der Dämmerung.
Der blaue Quell zu deinen Füßen, geheimnisvoll die rote
    Stille deines Munds,
Umdüstert vom Schlummer des Laubs, dem dunklen
    Gold verfallener Sonnenblumen.
Deine Lider sind schwer von Mohn und träumen leise
    auf meiner Stirne.
Sanfte Glocken durchzittern die Brust. Eine blaue Wolke
Ist dein Antlitz auf mich gesunken in der Dämmerung.

WAYFARING

At nightfall they carried the stranger
Into the room of the dead;
An odour of tar; the red plane tree's soft rustling;
Dark flight of jackdaws, the guard marched
    on the square.
The sun has sunk in black linen; forever
    this bygone evening returns.
In the next room the sister is playing a Schubert sonata.
So softly sinks her smile into the ruined fountain,
Which rustles bluish in the twilight. Oh how ancient
    our lineage.
Someone whispers below in the garden; someone has
    left this black heaven.
Aroma of apples on top of the cupboard. Grandmother
    is lighting the golden candles.

Oh, how mild is autumn. Softly our footsteps ring out
    in the old park
Beneath tall trees. Oh, how sober is the hyacinthine
    face of twilight.
The blue spring at your feet, mysterious your mouth's
    red stillness
Made sombre by the leaves slumber, the dark gold
    of decayed sunflowers.
Your lids are heavy with poppy and dream softly
    against my brow.
Gentle bells quiver in the breast. A blue cloud
Your face is sunk over me in the twilight.

Ein Lied zur Gitarre, das in einer fremden Schenke erklingt,
Die wilden Holunderbüsche dort, ein lang vergangener
Novembertag,
Vertraute Schritte auf der dämmernden Stiege, der
Anblick gebräunter Balken,
Ein offenes Fenster, an dem ein süßes Hoffen zurückblieb –
Unsäglich ist das alles, o Gott, daß man erschüttert ins
Knie bricht.

O, wie dunkel ist diese Nacht. Eine purpurne Flamme
Erlosch an meinem Mund. In der Stille
Erstirbt der bangen Seele einsames Saitenspiel.
Laß, wenn trunken von Wein das Haupt in die
Gosse sinkt.

A song for guitar rings out from an unknown tavern,
The wild elder bushes there, a long bygone
    November day,
Familiar steps on the dusking stairway, the sight of beams
    turned brown,
An open window, at which a sweet hope lingered –
Unspeakable it all is, Oh God one falls to one's knees
    overwhelmed.

Oh how dark is this night. A crimson flame
Died at my mouth. In the stillness
The anxious soul's lonely music fades to perish.
Enough, when drunk with wine the head sinks down
    into the gutter.

SEBASTIAN IM TRAUM
Für Adolf Loos

Mutter trug das Kindlein im weißen Mond,
Im Schatten des Nußbaums, uralten Holunders,
Trunken vom Safte des Mohns, der Klage der Drossel;
Und stille
Neigte in Mitleid sich über jene ein bärtiges Antlitz

Leise im Dunkel des Fensters; und altes Hausgerät
Der Väter
Lag im Verfall; Liebe und herbstliche Träumerei.

Also dunkel der Tag des Jahrs, traurige Kindheit,
Da der Knabe leise zu kühlen Wassern, silbernen Fischen
        hinabstieg,
Ruh und Antlitz;
Da er steinern sich vor rasende Rappen warf,
In grauer Nacht sein Stern über ihn kam;

Oder wenn er an der frierenden Hand der Mutter
Abends über Sankt Peters herbstlichen Friedhof ging
Ein zarter Leichnam stille im Dunkel der Kammer lag
Und jener die kalten Lider über ihn aufhob.

Er aber war ein kleiner Vogel im kahlen Geäst,
Die Glocke klang im Abendnovember,
Des Vaters Stille, da er im Schlaf die dämmernde
        Wendeltreppe hinabstieg.

Frieden der Seele. Einsamer Winterabend,
Die dunklen Gestalten der Hirten am alten Weiher;
Kindlein in der Hütte von Stroh; o wie leise
Sank in schwarzem Fieber das Antlitz hin.
Heilige Nacht.

SEBASTIAN IN DREAM

For Adolf Loos

Mother carried the child in the white moon,
In the nut tree's shadow, the ancient elder.
Drunk on poppy sap, the lament of the thrush;
And calmly
In sympathy a bearded face bowed down to her,

Quiet in the window's dark, and bygone belongings
Of the fathers
Lay mouldering; love and autumnal reverie.

Dark then was the day of the year, mournful childhood,
When softly the boy descended to cool waters,
        silver fishes,
Calm and countenance;
When stonily he launched himself before black horses
        galloping,
In the grey night his star rose over him.

Or at evening holding the icy hand of his mother
He passed through St Peters autumn churchyard,
A tender corpse lay still in the darkness of the chamber
And raised cold lids over him.

But he was a tiny bird in bare branches,
In evening November the bell sounded,
The Father's stillness, when in sleep he descended
        the darkening spiral stair.

Peace of the soul. Lonely winter evening.
The dark shapes of shepherds by the ancient pond;
Infant in the hut of straw; O how softly
Into black fever his face sank down.
Holy night.

Oder wenn er an der harten Hand des Vaters
Stille den finstern Kalvarienberg hinanstieg
Und in dämmernden Felsennischen
Die blaue Gestalt des Menschen durch seine Legende ging,
Aus der Wunde unter dem Herzen purpurn das Blut rann.
O wie leise stand in dunkler Seele das Kreuz auf.

Liebe; da in schwarzen Winkeln der Schnee schmolz,
Ein blaues Lüftchen sich heiter im alten Holunder fing,
In dem Schattengewölbe des Nußbaums;
Und dem Knaben leise sein rosiger Engel erschien;

Freude; da in kühlen Zimmern eine Abendsonate erklang
Im braunen Holzgebälk
Ein blauer Falter aus der silbernen Puppe kroch.

O die Nähe des Todes. In steinerner Mauer
Neigte sich ein gelbes Haupt, schweigend das Kind,
Da in jenem März der Mond verfiel.

Rosige Osterglocke im Grabgewölbe der Nacht
Und die Silberstimmen der Sterne,
Daß in Schauern ein dunkler Wahnsinn von der
    Stirne des Schläfers sank.

O wie stille ein Gang den blauen Fluß hinab
Vergessenes sinnend, da im grünen Geäst
Die Drossel ein Fremdes im den Untergang rief.

Or holding his father's hardened hand, in silence
He ascended dark Calvary.
And in shadowy rock niches
The blue form of man passed through his legend,
From the wound beneath his heart the crimson blood
     flowed out.
O how softly rose the cross in the darkness of his soul.

Love; when in black corners the snow melted,
Cheerfully a blue breeze caught in the ancient elder,
In the nut tree's vault of shadow
And softly to the boy appeared his rosy angel.

Joy; when in cool rooms an evening sonata sang out
From brown beams of wood
A blue moth crept from its silver chrysalis.

O the nearness of death. From stony walls
A yellow head bowed down, the child silent,
As in that March the moon decayed.

Rosy Easter bell in the tomb vault of night
And the stars, their silver voices,
As shuddering, a sombre madness sank from the
     sleeper's brow.

O how peaceful to pass down the blue river
Musing on that forgotten, when from verdant boughs
The thrush called a stranger into decline.

Oder wenn er an der knöchernen Hand des Greisen
Abends vor die verfallene Mauer der Stadt ging
Und jener in schwarzem Mantel ein rosiges Kindlein trug,
Im Schatten des Nußbaums der Geist des Bösen erschien.

Tasten über die grünen Stufen des Sommers. O wie
    leise
Verlief der Garten in der braunen Stille des Herbstes
Duft und Schwermut des alten Holunders,
Da in Sebastians Schatten die Silberstimme des Engels
    erstarb.

AM MOOR

Wanderer im schwarzen Wind; leise flüstert das dürre Rohr
In der Stille des Moors. Am grauen Himmel
Ein Zug von wilden Vögeln folgt;
Quere über finsteren Wassern.

Aufruhr. In verfallener Hütte
Aufflattert mit schwarzen Flügeln die Fäulnis;
Verkrüppelte Birken seufzen im Wind.

Abend in verlassener Schenke. Den Heimweg umwittert
Die sanfte Schwermut grasender Herden,
Erscheinung der Nacht: Kröten tauchen aus silbernen
    Wassern.

Or holding the bony hand of the old man
He went at evening to the crumbling city walls,
And in a black coat carried a rosy child,
In the nut tree's shade the spirit of evil appeared.

Feeling his way over the green steps of summer. O how
    softly
The garden decayed into brown autumn stillness,
Fragrance and melancholy of the ancient elder
When in Sebastian's shadow the silver voice of the angel
    died out.

ON THE MOOR

Wayfarer in black wind; softly whispers the withered reed
In the stillness of the moor. Against grey skies
A flight of wild fowl passes,
Cross-wise over dark waters.

Pandemonium. In a derelict hut
On black wings, decay flutters up;
Crippled birches sigh in the wind.

Evening in the deserted inn. The gentle melancholy
Of grazing herds enshrouds the way home,
Apparition of night: toads emerge from silvery waters.

RUH UND SCHWEIGEN

Hirten begruben die Sonne im kahlen Wald.
Ein Fischer zog
In härenem Netz den Mond aus frierendem Weiher.

In blauem Kristall
Wohnt der bleiche Mensch, die Wang' an seine
    Sterne gelehnt;
Oder er neigt das Haupt in purpurnem Schlaf.

Doch immer rührt der schwarze Flug der Vögel
Den Schauenden, das Heilige blauer Blumen,
Denkt die nahe Stille Vergessenes, erloschene Engel.

Wieder nachtet die Stirne in mondenem Gestein;
Ein strahlender Jüngling
Erscheint die Schwester in Herbst und schwarzer
    Verwesung.

REST AND SILENCE

Shepherds buried the sun in the bare forest.
A fisherman hauled
The moon in fine nets from the frozen pond.

In blue crystal
Pallid man dwells, cheek resting against his stars;
Or head inclined in crimson sleep.

But still he who gazes out is touched
By the birds' black flight, blue flowers and their holiness,
A closer stillness ponders the forgotten, angels extinguished.

Once more the brow grows dark in lunar stone;
A radiant youth
The sister appears in autumn and black corruption.

AM MÖNCHSBERG

Wo im Schatten herbstlicher Ulmen der verfallene Pfad
    hinabsinkt,
Ferne den Hütten von Laub, schlafenden Hirten,
Immer folgt dem Wandrer die dunkle Gestalt der Kühle

Über knöchernen Steg, die hyazinthene Stimme des
    Knaben,
Leise sagend die vergessene Legende des Walds,
Sanfter ein Krankes nun die wilde Klage des Bruders.

Also rührt ein spärliches Grün das Knie des Fremdlings,
Das versteinerte Haupt;
Näher rauscht der blaue Quell die Klage der Frauen.

ON THE MÖNCHSBERG

Where, in the shadow of autumn elms the decayed path
    sinks down,
Far from the huts of leaves, sleeping shepherds,
Always the dark form of coolness follows the wayfarer

Over the bridge of bone, the hyacinth voice of the boy
Softly chanting the forgotten legend of the woods.
And more gently a sick thing now, the brother's wild lament.

So a touch of green stirs the knee of the stranger
His hardening head;
Nearer the blue spring murmurs the women's lament.

KASPAR HAUSER LIED
Für Bessie Loos

Er wahrlich liebte die Sonne, die purpurn den Hügel
hinabstieg,
Die Wege des Walds, den singenden Schwarzvogel
Und die Freude des Grüns.

Ernsthaft war sein Wohnen im Schatten des Baums
Und rein sein Antlitz.
Gott sprach eine sanfte Flamme zu seinem Herzen:
O Mensch!

Stille fand sein Schritt die Stadt am Abend;
Die dunkle Klage seines Munds:
Ich will ein Reiter werden.

Ihm aber folgte Busch und Tier,
Haus und Dämmergarten weißer Menschen
Und sein Mörder suchte nach ihm.

Frühling und Sommer und schön der Herbst
Des Gerechten, sein leiser Schritt
An den dunklen Zimmern Träumender hin.
Nachts blieb er mit seinem Stern allein;

Sah, daß Schnee fiel in kahles Gezweig
Und im dämmernden Hausflur den Schatten des
Mörders.

Silbern sank des Ungebornen Haupt hin.

KASPAR HAUSER SONG

For Bessie Loos

Truly he loved the sun, as crimson it sank
     behind the hill,
The woodland paths, the blackbird's song,
The joy of the green.

Solemn was his dwelling in the tree's shadow
And pure his countenance.
Into his hand God spoke a gentle flame:
O Man!

Silent found his footfall the city at evening;
The dark lament of his mouth:
I want to be a horseman.

But bush and beast shadowed him,
House and darkened garden of white men
And his murderer stalked him.

Spring, summer and beautiful the autumn
Of the righteous one, his soft step
Outside the dark rooms of dreamers.
At night he remained alone with his star;

Saw snow falling through bare branches
And the murderer's shadow in the gloomy
     passage.

Silver sank the head of one unborn.

ENTLANG

Geschnitten sind Korn und Traube,
Der Weiler in Herbst und Ruh.
Hammer und Amboß klingt immerzu,
Lachen in purpurner Laube.

Astern von dunklen Zäunen
Bring dem weißen Kind.
Sag wie lang wir gestorben sind;
Sonne will schwarz erscheinen.

Rotes Fischlein im Weiher;
Stirn, die sich fürchtig belauscht;
Abendwind leise ans Fenster rauscht,
Blaues Orgelgeleier.

Stern und heimlich Gefunkel
Läßt noch einmal aufschaun.
Erscheinung der Mutter in Schmerz und Graun;
Schwarze Reseden im Dunkel.

ALONG

Corn and grape have been cut,
The hamlet in autumn and peace.
Hammer and anvil sound without cease,
Laughter in purple leaves.

Asters from dark fences
Bring to the white child.
Say how long we've been dead;
The sun will seem black.

Little red fish in the pond;
Forehead that fearful observes itself;
Softly the evening wind rustles at the window,
Blue organ drone.

Star and secret sparkle
Once more allows an upward gaze.
Advent of the mother in grief and horror;
Black mignonettes in the dark.

DER HERBST DES EINSAMEN

Der dunkle Herbst kehrt ein voll Frucht und Fülle,
Vergilbter Glanz von schönen Sommertagen.
Ein reines Blau tritt aus verfallner Hülle;
Der Flug der Vögel tönt von alten Sagen.
Gekeltert ist der Wein, die milde Stille
Erfüllt von leiser Antwort dunkler Fragen.

Und hier und dort ein Kreuz auf ödem Hügel;
Im roten Wald verliert sich eine Herde.
Die Wolke wandert übern Weiherspiegel;
Es ruht des Landmanns ruhige Geberde.
Sehr leise rührt des Abends blauer Flügel
Ein Dach von dürrem Stroh, die schwarze Erde.

Bald nisten Sterne in des Müden Brauen;
In kühle Stuben kehrt ein still Bescheiden
Und Engel treten leise aus den blauen
Augen der Liebenden, die sanfter leiden.
Es rauscht das Rohr; anfällt ein knöchern Grauen,
Wenn schwarz der Tau tropft von den kahlen Weiden.

AUTUMN OF THE SOLITARY

Dark autumn returns swollen with fruits and abundance,
The yellowing sheen of radiant summer days.
A pure blue steps from a shell decayed ;
The flight of birds resounds with bygone legends.
Wine is pressed, the gentle stillness
Fills with quiet answers to dark questions.

And here and there a cross on a desolate hill;
A herd fades away into red woods.
Above the pond mirror strays a cloud;
The farmer's quiet gesture comes to rest.
So softly stirs evening's blue flight
A roof of dry straw, the black earth.

Soon stars nestle in the brow of the weary one;
In cool rooms a quiet modesty returns
And angels step softly from the blue
Eyes of lovers who more calmly bear their torment.
Rustling of reeds; a bony horror attacks,
When from the bare willow bough black dew drips.

AN DIE VERSTUMMTEN

O, der Wahnsinn der großen Stadt, da am Abend
An schwarzer Mauer verkrüppelte Bäume starren,
Aus silberner Maske der Geist des Bösen schaut;
Licht mit magnetischer Geißel die steinerne Nacht verdrängt.
O, das versunkene Läuten der Abendglocken.

Hure, die in eisigen Schauern ein totes Kindlein gebärt.
Rasend peitscht Gottes Zorn die Stirn des Besessenen,
Purpurne Seuche, Hunger, der grüne Augen zerbricht.
O, das gräßliche Lachen des Golds.

Aber stille blutet in dunkler Höhle stummere Menschheit,
Fügt aus harten Metallen das erlösende Haupt.

TO THE SILENCED

O the insanity of the great city, where at nightfall
Against black walls the stunted trees stiffen,
The spirit of evil peers from a silver mask;
Light with magnetic scourge drives out the stony night.
O the sunken tolling of evening bells.

Whore, who bears a dead child in icy convulsions.
God's wrath with screaming whips over the brows of
        those possessed.
Purple plague, hunger, that ruptures green eyes,
O the gruesome laughter of gold.

But in dark caves a mankind more silent bleeds,
From hard metals forms the redeeming head.

AN EINEN FRÜHVERSTORBENEN

O, der schwarze Engel, der leise aus dem Innern des
    Baums trat,
Da wir sanfte Gespielen am Abend waren,
Am Rand des bläulichen Brunnens.
Ruhig war unser Schritt, die runden Augen in der braunen
    Kühle des Herbstes,
O, die purpurne Süße der Sterne.

Jener aber ging die steinernen Stufen des Mönchsbergs
    hinab,
Ein blaues Lächeln im Antlitz und seltsam verpuppt
In seine stillere Kindheit und starb;
Und im Garten blieb das silberne Antlitz des Freundes zurück,
Lauschend im Laub oder im alten Gestein.

Seele sang den Tod, die grüne Verwesung des Fleisches
Und es war das Rauschen des Walds,
Die inbrünstige Klage des Wildes.
Immer klangen von dämmernden Türmen die blauen
    Glocken des Abends.

Stunde kam, da jener die Schatten in purpurner Sonne sah,
Die Schatten der Fäulnis in kahlem Geäst;
Abend, da an dämmernder Mauer die Amsel sang,
Der Geist des Frühverstorbenen stille im Zimmer erschien.

O, das Blut, das aus der Kehle des Tönenden rinnt,
Blaue Blume; o die feurige Träne
Geweint in die Nacht.

Goldene Wolke und Zeit. In einsamer Kammer
Lädst du öfter den Toten zu Gast,
Wandelst in trautem Gespräch unter Ulmen den grünen
    Fluss hinab.

TO ONE WHO DIED YOUNG

Oh, the black angel, who stepped softly from the
        heart of the tree
When we were gentle playmates in the evening,
At the edge of the bluish fountain.
Peaceful was our footfall, eyes round in the
        brown coolness of autumn,
Oh the purple sweetness of the stars.

But one who descended the stone steps of the Mönchsberg,
A blue smile on his face and strangely cocooned
In his calmer childhood, died;
And in the garden the wind's silver face
        remained behind,
Listening in the leaves, in old stones.

Soul sang of death, green decay of the flesh,
And it was the stirring of the forest,
The ardent lament of game.
Always from the towers at dusk the blue evening bells
        rang out.

The hour came when he saw shadows in the crimson sun,
Shadows of corruption in bare branches;
At evening, when by dusking walls the blackbird sang,
Silently in the room appeared the spirit of one who died young.

Oh, blood that drains from the throat of the sound maker
Blue flower; oh the fiery tears
Wept into night.

Golden cloud and time. In a lonely room
You request a visit from the dead one often,
You stroll beneath elms down the green river
        enveloped in warm conversation.

GEBURT

Gebirge: Schwärze, Schweigen und Schnee.
Rot vom Wald niedersteigt die Jagd;
O, die moosigen Blicke des Wilds.

Stille der Mutter; unter schwarzen Tannen
Öffnen sich die schlafenden Hände,
Wenn verfallen der kalte Mond erscheint.

O, die Geburt des Menschen. Nächtlich rauscht
Blaues Wasser im Felsengrund;
Seufzend erblickt sein Bild der gefallene Engel,

Erwacht ein Bleiches in dumpfer Stube.
Zwei Monde
Erglänzen die Augen der steinernen Greisin.

Weh, der Gebärenden Schrei. Mit schwarzem Flügel
Rührt die Knabenschläfe die Nacht,
Schnee, der leise aus purpurner Wolke sinkt.

BIRTH

Mountain range: blackness, silence, snow.
Red from the forest the hunt descends;
Oh, the mossy glances of the deer.

Stillness of the mother; beneath black pines
The sleeping hands unfold
When in decay the cold moon appears.

Oh, the birth of man. Nightly the blue waters
Roar over the bed of rocks,
Sighing the fallen angel beholds his image,

A pale thing wakes in the musty room.
Two moons
The eyes of the old stone woman are shining.

Oh, pain, the scream of labour. With black wings
Night caresses the boy's temples,
Snow, softly sinking from crimson cloud.

DER WANDERER

Immer lehnt am Hügel die weiße Nacht,
Wo in Silbertönen die Pappel ragt,
Stern' und Steine sind.

Schlafend wölbt sich über den Gießbach der Steg,
Folgt dem Knaben ein erstorbenes Antlitz,
Sichelmond in rosiger Schlucht

Ferne preisenden Hirten. In altem Gestein
Schaut aus kristallenen Augen die Kröte,
Erwacht der blühende Wind, die Vogelstimme des
        Totengleichen
Und die Schritte ergrünen leise im Wald.

Dieses erinnert an Baum und Tier. Langsame Stufen von Moos;
Und der Mond,
Der glänzend in traurigen Wassern versinkt.

Jener kehrt wieder und wandelt an grünem Gestade,
Schaukelt auf schwarzem Gondelschiffchen durch die
        verfallene Stadt.

THE WAYFARER

Ever the white night leans against the hill,
Where in silver sound the poplar looms,
Star and stone can be found.

Sleeping the path arches over the torrent,
A dead face follows the boy,
And crescent moon in the rosy ravine

Shepherds praising far off. In old rocks
The toads gaze out with crystal eyes,
The blossoming wind awakes, the bird voice
    of one as dead
And steps green softly in the wood.

These recall tree and beast. Slow steps of moss;
And the moon,
That glowing sinks into mournful waters.

He returns again and strolls to the green strand,
Rocking on black gondolas through the
    decayed city.

DIE SONNE

Täglich kommt die gelbe Sonne über den Hügel.
Schön ist der Wald, das dunkle Tier,
Der Mensch; Jäger oder Hirt.

Rötlich steigt im grünen Weiher der Fisch.
Unter dem runden Himmel
Fährt der Fischer leise im blauen Kahn.

Langsam reift die Traube, das Korn.
Wenn sich stille der Tag neigt,
Ist ein Gutes und Böses bereitet.

Wenn es Nacht wird,
Hebt der Wanderer leise die schweren Lider;
Sonne aus finsterer Schlucht bricht.

THE SUN

Daily the sun comes over the hill.
Beautiful is the forest, the dark beast,
Man, hunter or shepherd.

Ruddy rises the fish in the green pond.
Beneath rounded skies
The fisherman moves softly in a blue boat.

Slowly ripens the grape, the corn.
As day closes in stillness,
A good and an evil is prepared.

When night comes
The wayfarer softly lifts his heavy lids;
Sun breaks from a dark abyss.

FÖHN

Blinde Klage im Wind, mondene Wintertage,
Kindheit, leise verhallen die Schritte an schwarzer Hecke
Langes Abendgeläut.
Leise kommt die weiße Nacht gezogen,

Verwandelt in purpurne Träume Schmerz und Plage
Des steinigen Lebens,
Daß nimmer der dornige Stachel ablasse vom
verwesenden Leib.

Tief im Schlummer aufseufzt die bange Seele,

Tief der Wind in zerbrochenen Bäumen,
Und es schwankt die Klagegestalt
Der Mutter durch den einsamen Wald

Dieser schweigenden Trauer; Nächte,
Erfüllt von Tränen, feurigen Engeln.
Silbern zerschellt an kahler Mauer ein kindlich Gerippe.

FÖHN

Blind lament in the wind, lunar winter days,
Childhood, softly footsteps fade by the black hedge,
Long chime of evening.
Softly the white night slinks in,

Turns to crimson dreams the pain and plague
Of stony life,
That never may the thorny barb relent from
    the decaying body.

Deep in slumber sighs the anxious soul.

Deep the wind in shattered trees
And the lamenting figure of the mother
Sways through the lonely wood

Of this speechless grief; nights
Filled with tears and angels afire.
Silver, against bare walls a child skeleton shatters.

WINTERNACHT

Es ist Schnee gefallen. Nach Mitternacht verlässt du betrunken von purpurnem Wein den dunklen Bezirk der Menschen, die rote Flamme ihres Herdes. O die Finsternis!

Schwarzer Frost. Die Erde ist hart, nach Bitterem schmeckt die Luft. Deine Sterne schließen sich zu bösen Zeichen.

Mit versteinerten Schritten stampfst du am Bahndamm hin, mit runden Augen, wie ein Soldat, der eine schwarze Schanze stürmt. Avanti!

Bitterer Schnee und Mond!

Ein roter Wolf, den ein Engel würgt. Deine Beine klirren schreitend wie blaues Eis und ein Lächeln voll Trauer und Hochmut hat dein Antlitz versteinert und die Stirne erbleicht vor der Wollust des Frostes;

oder sie neigt sich schweigend über den Schlaf eines Wächters, der in seiner hölzernen Hütte hinsank.

Frost und Rauch. Ein weißes Sternenhemd vebrennt die tragenden Schultern und Gottes Geier zerfleischen dein metallenes Herz.

O der steinerne Hügel. Stille schmilzt und vergessen der külhle Leib im silbernen Schnee hin.

Schwarz ist der Schlaf. Das Ohr folgt lange den Pfaden der Sterne im Eis.

Beim Erwachen klangen die Glocken im Dorf. Aus dem östlichen Tor trat silbern der rosige Tag.

WINTER NIGHT

Snow has fallen. After midnight drunk on purple wine, you depart the dark district of men, the red flame of their hearth. Oh darkness!

Black frost. The earth is hard, the air tastes of bitterness. Your stars conspire to form evil signs.

With petrified steps you stamp along the embankment, eyes like discs, those of a soldier storming a dark trench. Avanti!

Bitter the snow and moon!

A red wolf which an angel is strangling. Your marching legs jangle like blue ice and a smile filled with sorrow and pride has petrified your face and your brow pales in the lust of the frost;

or silently inclines over the sleep of a watchman who sank down in his wooden hut.

Frost and smoke. A shirt of white stars burns the wearers' shoulders, and God's vultures tear into your metal heart.

O the stony hill. Peaceful and forgotten, the cool body melts away in silver snow.

Black is sleep. Far into the ice the ear shadows the path of stars.

When you awoke the village bells were ringing.The rosy day stepped silver through the eastern gate.

IN VENEDIG

Stille in nächtigem Zimmer.
Silbern flackert der Leuchter
Vor dem singenden Odem
Des Einsamen;
Zaubrisches Rosengewölk.

Schwärzlicher Fliegenschwarm
Verdunkelt den steinernen Raum
Und es starrt von der Qual
Des goldenen Tags das Haupt
Des Heimatlosen.

Reglos nachtet das Meer.
Stern und schwärzliche Fahrt
Entschwand am Kanal.
Kind, dein kränkliches Lächeln
Folgte mir leise im Schlaf.

IN VENICE

Stillness in the room at night
The candlestick flickers silver
Before the singing breath
Of the lonely one;
Enchanted rose-clouds.

Black fly swarms
Darken the stone space
And from the agony of golden days
Stares the head of the homeless one.

The sea comes to rest at night.
Star and black voyage
Vanish on the canal.
Child, your sickly smile
Shadowed me softly into sleep.

SOMMER

Am Abend schweigt die Klage
Des Kuckucks im Wald.
Tiefer neigt sich das Korn,
Der rote Mohn.

Schwarzes Gewitter droht
Über dem Hügel.
Das alte Lied der Grille
Erstirbt im Feld.

Nimmer regt sich das Laub
Der Kastanie.
Auf der Wendeltreppe
Rauscht dein Kleid.

Stille leuchtet die Kerze
Im dunklen Zimmer;
Eine silberne Hand
Löschte sie aus;

Windstille, sternlose Nacht.

SUMMER

At evening the cuckoo's lament
Falls silent in the wood.
Deeper bends the corn,
The red poppy.

Black thunder threatens
Above the hill.
The ancient song of the cricket
Fades out in the field.

The leaves of the chestnut
Stir no more.
On the spiral staircase
Your dress rustles.

A candle's stillness shines
In the dark room;
Snuffed out
By a silvery hand;

Windless, starless night.

SOMMERSNEIGE

Der grüne Sommer ist so leise
Geworden, dein kristallenes Antlitz.
Am Abendweiher starben die Blumen,
Ein erschrockener Amselruf.

Vergebliche Hoffnung des Lebens. Schon rüstet
Zur Reise sich die Schwalbe im Haus
Und die Sonne versinkt am Hügel;
Schon winkt zur Sternenreise die Nacht.

Stille der Dörfer; es tönen rings
Die verlassenen Wälder. Herz,
Neige dich nun liebender
Über die ruhige Schläferin.

Der grüne Sommer ist so leise
Geworden und es läutet der Schritt
Des Fremdlings durch die silberne Nacht.
Gedächte ein blaues Wild seines Pfads,

Des Wohllauts seiner geistlichen Jahre!

CLOSE OF SUMMER

The green summer has turned so still,
Your crystal face.
By the evening pond the flowers died,
The blackbird's startled call.

Futile hope of life. Already the swallow
Prepares for its journey
And the sun sinks down behind the hill;
Night beckons on its own star journey.

The stillness of villages; all around
The deserted woods resound. Heart,
Incline more lovingly
Over the peaceful sleeping woman.

The green summer has turned so still
And the steps of the stranger ring out
Through the silver night.
Should blue game recall its path,

The harmonious sound of its holy year!

JAHR

Dunkle Stille der Kindheit. Unter grünenden Eschen
Weidet die Sanftmut bläulichen Blickes; goldene Ruh.
Ein Dunkles entzückt der Duft der Veilchen;
    schwankende Ähren
Im Abend, Samen und die goldenen Schatten der
    Schwermut.
Balken behaut der Zimmermann; im dämmernden Grund
Mahlt die Mühle; im Hasellaub wölbt sich ein
    purpurner Mund,
Männliches rot über schweigende Wasser geneigt.
Leise ist der Herbst, der Geist des Waldes; goldene Wolke
Folgt dem Einsamen, der schwarze Schatten des Enkels.
Neige in steinernem Zimmer; unter alten Zypressen
Sind der Tränen nächtige Bilder zum Quell versammelt;
Goldenes Auge des Anbeginns, dunkle Geduld des
    Endes.

YEAR

Dark stillness of childhood. Beneath greening ash trees
Grazes gentleness of a bluish glance, golden peace.
A dark thing delights in the scent of violets;
    swaying corn.
At evening, seed and the golden shadows of
    melancholy.
The carpenter hews the beam, on shadowy ground
The mill grinds; in the leaves of the hazel arches a
    crimson mouth,
Masculine red bowed over silent waters.
Soft is autumn, spirit of the woods; golden cloud
Follows the solitary, the black shadow of the descendant.
Fading out in stony rooms; beneath old cypresses
Nightly images of tears gather at the source;
Golden eye of beginning, dark patience of
    the end.

ABENDLAND
Else Lasker-Schüler in Verehrung

I

Mond, als träte ein Totes
Aus blauer Höhle,
Und es fallen der Blüten
Viele über den Felsenpfad.
Silbern weint ein Krankes
Am Abendweiher,
Auf schwarzem Kahn
Hinüberstarben Liebende.

Oder es läuten die Schritte
Elis' durch den Hain
Den hyazinthenen
Wieder verhallend unter Eichen.
O des Knaben Gestalt
Geformt aus kristallenen Tränen,
Nächtigen Schatten.
Zackige Blitze erhellen die Schläfe
Die immerkühle,
Wenn am grünenden Hügel
Frühlingsgewitter ertönt.

II

So leise sind die grünen Wälder
Unsrer Heimat,
Die kristallne Woge
Hinsterbend an verfallner Mauer
Und wir haben im Schlaf geweint;

THE WEST

In honour of Else Lasker-Schüler

I

Moon, as though a dead one
Stepped from a blue cavern,
And the blossoms fell in number
Across the rocky path.
Silver weeps a sick one
By the evening pond,
In a little black boat
The lovers passed over to death.

Or the footsteps of Elis
Ring through the grove,
The hyacinthine
Dying again beneath the oaks.
O the form of that boy
Conceived from crystal tears,
Nocturnal shadows,
Jagged lightning livened his temples
The ever-cool,
When on the greening hill
Springtime storms resound.

II

So quiet are the green woods
Of our homeland,
The crystal wave
Dying against the ruined wall,
And we have wept in sleep;

Wandern mit zögernden Schritten
An der dornigen Hecke hin
Singende im Abendsommer,
In heiliger Ruh
Des fern verstrahlenden Weinbergs;
Schatten nun im kühlen Schoss
Der Nacht, trauernde Adler.
So leise schliesst ein mondener Strahl
Die purpurnen Male der Schwermut.

III

Ihr grossen Städte
Steinern aufgebaut
In der Ebene!
So sprachlos folgt
Der Heimatlose
Mit dunkler Stirne dem Wind,
Kahlen Bäumen am Hügel.
Ihr weithin dämmernden Ströme!
Gewaltig ängstet
Schaurige Abendröte
Im Sturmgewölk.
Ihr sterbenden Völker!
Bleiche Woge
Zerschellend am Strande der Nacht,
Fallende Sterne.

Along the thorny hedgerow
Singers wander, footsteps wavering
In the evening summer,
In holy peace
Of the vineyard's distant shimmering;
Shadows now in the cool bosom
Of night, eagles mourning.
So gently a moonbeam closes
Crimson marks of melancholy.

III

You giant cities
Raised in stone
Upon the plain!
So dumbstruck
And with darkened brow
The exiled follows the wind,
Bare trees upon the hill.
You rivers dusking in the distance!
A gruesome sunset
endures dread fear
among the storm clouds.
You dying peoples!
Ashen wave
Shattered on the shore of night,
Stars falling.

GESANG EINER GEFANGENEN AMSEL

Für Ludwig von Ficker

Dunkler Odem im grünen Gezweig.
Blaue Blümchen umschweben das Antlitz
Des Einsamen, den goldenen Schritt
Ersterbend unter dem Ölbaum.
Aufflattert mit trunknem Flügel die Nacht.
So leise blutet Demut,
Tau, der langsam tropft vom blühenden Dorn.
Strahlender Arme Erbarmen
Umfängt ein brechendes Herz.

SONG OF A CAPTIVE BLACKBIRD

For Ludwig von Ficker

Dark breath in green branches.
Blue flowers float before the face
Of the solitary, the golden footfall
Dying away beneath the olive tree.
On drunken wing night flutters up.
So softly bleeds humility,
Dew, that drips from the blossoming thorn.
The compassion of radiant arms
Envelops a breaking heart.

VORHÖLLE

An herbstlichen Mauern, es suchen Schatten dort
Am Hügel das tönende Gold
Weidende Abendwolken
In der Ruh verdorrter Platanen.
Dunklere Tränen odmet diese Zeit,
Verdammnis, da des Träumers Herz
Überfließt von purpurner Abendröte,
Der Schwermut der rauchenden Stadt;
Dem Schreitenden nachweht goldene Kühle,
Dem Fremdling, vom Friedhof,
Als folgte im Schatten ein zarter Leichnam.

Leise läutet der steinerne Bau;
Der Garten der Waisen, das dunkle Spital,
Ein rotes Schiff am Kanal.
Träumend steigen und sinken im Dunkel
Verwesende Menschen
Und aus schwärzlichen Toren
Treten Engel mit kalten Stirnen hervor;
Bläue, die Todesklagen der Mütter.
Es rollt durch ihr langes Haar,
Ein feuriges Rad, der runde Tag
Der Erde Qual ohne Ende.

In kühlen Zimmern ohne Sinn
Modert Gerät, mit knöchernen Händen
Tastet im Blau nach Märchen
Unheilige Kindheit,
Benagt die fette Ratte Tür und Truh,
Ein Herz
Erstarrt in schneeiger Stille.
Nachhallen die purpurnen Flüche
Des Hungers in faulendem Dunkel,
Die schwarzen Schwerter der Lüge,
Als schlüge zusammen ein ehernes Tor.

LIMBO

By autumnal walls, there shadows are searching
Ringing gold upon the hill,
Evening clouds that graze
In the withered plane trees' calm.
Darker tears this age exhales,
Damnation, when the dreamer's heart
Overflows with crimson sunset,
Melancholy of the smoking town;
Golden coolness blows behind the walker,
The stranger, from the graveyard,
As though a tender corpse followed in the shadows.

Softly chimes the stone building;
The orphans' garden, the dark hospital,
A red ship on the canal.
Dreaming rise and fall in darkness
Decaying men
And from blackish doorways
Angels step with icy brows;
Blueness, the death lament of mothers.
Through their long hair rolls
A fiery wheel, the round day
Earth agony without end.

In cool rooms without meaning,
Belongings moulder, with bony hands
Unholy childhood
Gropes in the blue for fairytales,
The fat rat gnaws coffer and door,
A heart
Stiffens in snowy silence.
The crimson curses of hunger resound
In decaying darkness,
The black sword of lies,
As though a brazen gate slammed shut.

DAS HERZ

Das wilde Herz ward weiß am Wald;
O dunkle Angst
Des Todes, so das Gold
In grauer Wolke starb.
Novemberabend.
Am kahlen Tor am Schlachthaus stand
Der armen Frauen Schar;
In jeden Korb
Fiel faules Fleisch und Eingeweid;
Verfluchte Kost!

Des Abends blaue Taube
Brachte nicht Versöhnung.
Dunkler Trompetenruf
Durchfuhr der Ulmen
Nasses Goldlaub,
Eine zerfetzte Fahne
Vom Blute rauchend,
Daß in wilder Schwermut
Hinlauscht ein Mann.
O! ihr ehernen Zeiten
Begraben dort im Abendrot.

Aus dunklem Hausflur trat
Die goldne Gestalt
Der Jünglingin
Umgeben von bleichen Monden,
Herbstlicher Hofstaat,
Zerknickten schwarze Tannen
Im Nachtsturm,
Die steile Festung,
O Herz
Hinüberschimmernd in schneeige Kühle.

THE HEART

The wild heart turned white in the wood;
O dark dread
Of death, so the gold
Perished in a grey cloud.
November evening.
At the stark gate of the slaughterhouse
Stood the throng of pauper women;
Into every basket
Putrid flesh and entrails fell;
Accursed fare!

The blue dove of evening
Brought no atonement.
Dark call of trumpets
Passed through the elms
Damp golden leaf,
A tattered banner
Smoking with blood,
To which in wild melancholy
A man hearkens.
O you brazen times
Buried there in the sun's embers.

From the darkened hallway stepped
The golden form
Of the young maiden
Enclosed by ashen moons,
Autumnal courtiers,
Black firs felled
In the night storm,
The sheer fortress.
O heart
Shimmering into snowy coolness.

DIE SCHWERMUT

Gewaltig bist du dunkler Mund
Im Innern, aus Herbstgewölk
Geformte Gestalt,
Goldner Abendstille;
Ein grünlich dämmernder Bergstrom
In zerbrochenen Föhren
Schattenbezirk;
Ein Dorf,
Das fromm in braunen Bildern abstirbt.

Da springen die schwarzen Pferde
Auf nebliger Weide.
Ihr Soldaten!
Vom Hügel, wo sterbend die Sonne rollt,
Stürzt das lachende Blut –
Unter Eichen
Sprachlos! O grollende Schwermut
Des Heers; ein strahlender Helm
Sank klirrend von purpurner Stirne.

Herbstesnacht so kühle kommt,
Erglänzt mit Sternen
Über zerbrochenem Männergebein
Die stille Mönchin.

MELANCHOLY

Mighty are you dark mouth
From within, figure formed
Of autumn clouds,
Golden evening stillness;
A greenish darkening mountain torrent
In shattered pine
Shadow district;
A village,
That decays devoutly in brown images.

There black horses frisk
On the misty pasture.
You soldiers!
From the hill, where the sun rolls dying,
Plunges the laughing blood –
Beneath oaks
Dumbstruck! O bitter melancholy
Of the army; a shining helmet
Sank clanking from the crimson brow.

Autumn night so cool advances,
Gleaming with stars
Over the shattered remains of men
The peaceful maiden monk.

DIE HEIMKEHR

Die Kühle dunkler Jahre,
Schmerz und Hoffnung
Bewahrt zyklopisch Gestein,
Menschenleeres Gebirge,
Des Herbstes goldner Odem,
Abendwolke –
Reinheit!

Anschaut aus blauen Augen
Kristallne Kindheit;
Unter dunklen Fichten
Liebe, Hoffnung,
Da von feurigen Lidern
Tau ins starre Gras tropft –
Unaufhaltsam!

O! dort der goldene Steg
Zerbrechend im Schnee
Des Abgrunds!
Blaue Kühle
Odmet das nächtige Tal,
Glaube, Hoffnung!
Gegrüßt du einsamer Friedhof!

HOMECOMING

Coolness of the dark year,
Suffering and hope
Preserved in cyclopean stone,
Mountains free of men,
Golden breath of autumn,
Evening cloud –
Purity!

From blue eyes
Crystal childhood gazes out;
Beneath dark spruce
Love, hope,
Thus from fiery lids
Into bristling grass, dew drips
Inexorably!

O! and there the golden bridge
Shattering in the snow
Of the abyss!
Blue coolness
Breathes the valley at night,
Faith, hope!
Greetings you lonely graveyard!

DER ABEND

Mit toten Heldengestalten
Erfüllst du Mond
Die schweigenden Wälder,
Sichelmond –
Mit der sanften Umarmung
Der Liebenden,
Den Schatten berühmter Zeiten
Die modernden Felsen rings;
So bläulich erstrahlt es
Gegen die Stadt hin,
Wo kalt und böse
Ein verwesend Geschlecht wohnt,
Der weißen Enkel
Dunkle Zukunft bereitet.
Ihr mondverschlungnen Schatten
Aufseufzend im leeren Kristall
Des Bergsees.

EVENING

With dead hero forms
Moon you are filling
The silent forests,
Crescent moon –
With the gentle embrace
Of lovers,
The shades of a famous age
The mouldering rocks all around;
So bluish it shines
Towards the town,
Where cold and evil
A species dwells in decline,
Grooming a dark future
For the white descendants.
You shadows moon-tangled
Sighing in the crystal void
Of the mountain lake.

DIE NACHT

Dich sing ich wilde Zerklüftung,
Im Nachtsturm
Aufgetürmtes Gebirge;
Ihr grauen Türme
Überfließend von höllischen Fratzen,
Feurigem Getier,
Rauhen Farnen, Fichten,
Kristallnen Blumen.
Unendliche Qual,
Daß du Gott erjagtest
Sanfter Geist,
Aufseufzend im Wassersturz,
In wogenden Föhren.

Golden lodern die Feuer
Der Völker rings.
Über schwärzliche Klippen
Stürzt todestrunken
Die erglühende Windsbraut,
Die blaue Woge
Des Gletschers
Und es dröhnt
Gewaltig die Glocke im Tal:
Flammen, Flüche
Und die dunklen
Spiele der Wollust,
Stürmt den Himmel
Ein versteinertes Haupt.

NIGHT

I sing you wild fissure,
In the night storm
Soaring mountains;
You grey towers
Spilling with hellish grimaces,
Animals aflame,
Harsh ferns, spruces,
Crystal flowers.
Agony everlasting,
That you hunt for God
Tender spirit,
Sighing in the falls,
Amongst the surging pines.

Golden flares the fire
About the gathered peoples.
Above blackish outcrops
Drunk with death
Plunges the glowing wind bride,
The blue surge
Of the glacier
And powerfully sounds the bell
In the valley:
Flames, curses
And the dark play of lust,
A hardened head
Storms heaven.

IN HELLBRUNN

Wieder folgend der blauen Klage des Abends
Am Hügel hin, am Frühlingsweiher –
Als schwebten darüber die Schatten lange Verstorbener,
Die Schatten der Kirchenfürsten, edler Frauen –
Schon blühen ihre Blumen, die ernsten Veilchen
Im Abendgrund, rauscht des blauen Quells
Kristallne Woge. So geistlich ergrünen
Die Eichen über den vergessenen Pfaden der Toten,
Die goldene Wolke über dem Weiher.

IN HELLBRUNN

Ever shadowing the blue lament of evening
Along the hill, the springtime pond –
As though the shades of those long deceased
The bishops and noblewomen floated over them –
Already their flowers bloom, earnest violets
In evening's abyss, crystal wave of the blue source
Rushing on. With such devotion grow
The greening oaks over the forgotten paths of the dead,
The golden cloud over the pond.

KLAGE (I)

Jüngling aus kristallnem Munde
Sank dein goldner Blick ins Tal;
Waldes Woge rot und fahl
In der schwarzen Abendstunde.
Abend schlägt so tiefe Wunde!

Angst! des Todes Traumbeschwerde,
Abgestorben Grab und gar
Schaut aus Baum und Wild das Jahr;
Kahles Feld und Ackererde,
Ruft der Hirt die bange Herde.

Schwester, deine blauen Brauen
Winken leise in der Nacht.
Orgel seufzt und Hölle lacht
Und es faßt das Herz ein Grauen;
Möchte Stern und Engel schauen.

Mutter muß ums Kindlein zagen;
Rot ertönt im Schacht das Erz,
Wollust, Tränen, steinern Schmerz,
Der Titanen dunkle Sagen.
Schwermut! einsam Adler klagen.

LAMENT (I)

Youth from a crystal mouth
Into the valley sinks your golden glance;
Red and pale the forest's surge
In the black evening hour.
Evening strikes so deep a wound!

Fear! Of death's dream complaint,
Lifeless grave and stark the year
Gazes out from tree and deer;
Bare field and farmed earth.
The boy calls in his fearful herd.

Sister, your blue eyebrows
Beckon softly in the night.
Organs sigh and hell laughs
And a horror seizes the heart;
Should one gaze on stars and angels.

Mother wavers before her infant;
Red sounds the ore down the shaft,
Lust, tears and stony pain,
Dark legends of the titans.
Melancholy! The lonely eagle's lament.

NACHTERGEBUNG

Mönchin! schließ mich in dein Dunkel,
Ihr Gebirge kühl und blau!
Niederblutet dunkler Tau;
Kreuz ragt steil im Sterngefunkel.

Purpurn brachen Mund und Lüge
In verfallner Kammer kühl;
Scheint noch Lachen, golden Spiel,
Einer Glocke letzte Züge.

Mondeswolke! Schwärzlich fallen
Wilde Früchte nachts vom Baum
Und zum Grabe wird der Raum
Und zum Traum dies Erdenwallen.

IM OSTEN

Den wilden Orgeln des Wintersturms
Gleicht des Volkes finstrer Zorn,
Die purpurne Woge der Schlacht,
Entlaubter Sterne.

Mit zerbrochnen Brauen, silbernen Armen
Winkt sterbenden Soldaten die Nacht.
Im Schatten der herbstlichen Esche
Seufzen die Geister der Erschlagenen.

Dornige Wildnis umgürtet die Stadt.
Von blutenden Stufen jagt der Mond
Die erschrockenen Frauen.
Wilde Wölfe brachen durchs Tor.

SURRENDER TO NIGHT

Monk woman! Seal me in your darkness,
Your mountains cool and blue!
Down bleeds the dark dew
Sheer climb of the cross in glittering stars.

Crimson breaks mouth and lie
In the cool and fading chamber;
Still laughter shimmers, golden play,
A bell's last labour.

Moon cloud! Blackly falls the wild fruit
From the tree at night
On to the grave goes space
And into dream this earthly passage.

IN THE EAST

Dark is the wrath of the people,
Like the wild organs of winter storm,
And the crimson wave of battle
Stripped leaf stars.

With shattered brows and silver arms
The night beckons dying soldiers.
In the shade of the autumn ash
The spirits of the slain are sighing.

Thorny wilderness girdles the city.
From blood-drenched steps the moon
Chases the terrified women.
Wild wolves have broken through the gate.

KLAGE (II)

Schlaf und Tod, die düstern Adler
Umrauschen nachtlang dieses Haupt:
Des Menschen goldnes Bildnis
Verschlänge die eisige Woge
Der Ewigkeit. An schaurigen Riffen
Zerschellt der purpurne Leib.
Und es klagt die dunkle Stimme
Über dem Meer.
Schwester stürmischer Schwermut
Sieh ein ängstlicher Kahn versinkt
Unter Sternen,
Dem schweigenden Antlitz der Nacht.

LAMENT (II)

The dark eagles, sleep and death
Night long sweep around this head:
Eternity's icy wave
Would devour man's golden image.
Against terrible reefs
His purple frame is smashed.
And the dark voice laments
Over the sea.
Sister of stormy melancholy,
Look a troubled boat sinks down
Under stars,
The silent countenance of night.

GRODEK

Am Abend tönen die herbstlichen Wälder
Von tödlichen Waffen, die goldnen Ebenen
Und blauen Seen, darüber die Sonne
Düstrer hinrollt; umfängt die Nacht
Sterbende Krieger, die wilde Klage
Ihrer zerbrochenen Münder.
Doch stille sammelt im Weidengrund
Rotes Gewölk, darin ein zürnender Gott wohnt,
Das vergossne Blut sich, mondne Kühle;
Alle Straßen münden in schwarze Verwesung.
Unter goldnem Gezweig der Nacht und Sternen
Es schwankt der Schwester Schatten durch den
        schweigenden Hain,
Zu grüßen die Geister der Helden, die blutenden Häupter;
Und leise tönen im Rohr die dunklen Flöten des Herbstes.
O stolzere Trauer! ihr ehernen Altäre,
Die heiße Flamme des Geistes nährt heute ein gewaltiger
        Schmerz,
Die ungebornen Enkel.

152

GRODEK

At nightfall the autumn woods resound
With deadly weapons,
The blue lakes and golden plains
Above which darkly the sun rolls down;
The night embraces dying warriors,
The wild lament of their broken mouths.
But calmly on the grazing land
Red clouds, in which a wrathful god resides,
The spilt blood collects, lunar coolness;
All roads lead to black putrefaction.
Beneath golden shoots of night and stars
The sister's shadow sways through the silent grove,
To greet the ghosts of the heroes, the bleeding heads;
And softly in the reeds sound the dark flutes of autumn.
O prouder grief! You brazen altars,
Today a mighty agony feeds the hot flame of the spirit,
The grandson still unborn.

TRAKL IN SALZBURG

Salzburg today is still a beautiful and beguiling city which profits from both an enviable geographical location and the retention of its oldest quarters more or less unscathed by war and brutal architectural intrusion. Visitors may spend several pleasant days strolling the lanes and squares which fan out from the cathedral or 'Dom'. They will be drawn to take the funicular up to the brooding fortress on the Mönchsberg, the sheer wall of rock that abruptly rears up to dominate the town and they will inevitably cross the muddied turquoise waters of the Salzach to walk through the refined landscapes of the famous Mirabell Gardens. Many are also in Salzburg of course to pay homage to its most famous son, Mozart. It's impossible to escape his presence, whether passing his imposing statue on the square named after him, hearing recitals of his music leaking from music rooms and chapels in the old town, or when meeting waves of his admirers of all nations moving relentlessly between his former residencies. But it is Mozart himself who inadvertently points one in the direction of Salzburg's lesser known artist son, who, although displaying a much less overt presence, is nevertheless commemorated at various locations across the city.

The Mozart statue

155

If one happens to stand beneath Mozart on his plinth and follow his gaze across the little square one will observe the café Glockenspiel, one of the most popular in Salzburg. A century ago this was the impressive residence of the Trakl family, a building which befitted the comfortable bourgeois lifestyle of Tobias, Maria and their children. Georg's bedroom was on the first floor, the third window from the left as one faces the café. So, when the youthful Trakl gazed out from his room he would have met the challenging stare of Mozart. Beyond, on the other side of the Salzach, rise the densely wooded slopes of the Kapuzinerberg, sister hill to the Mönchsberg, which together protectively enclose the town. Here the walls of the Capuchin monastery circumnavigate the slopes, their turreted towers peering through the firs and deciduous woodland at intervals. Beyond is the Gaisberg, the highest hill in Salzburg, from whose summit a breathtaking view of the city is assured. The Gaisberg was a constant reassuring presence in Trakl's early life since it could also be glimpsed from the balcony of the house where he was born, just around the corner from the residence on Mozart Platz. Although Trakl would prove notoriously ambiguous in his feelings towards his native city in later years and was capable of launching into venomous tirades against it, he felt a nostalgic longing for its romantic setting when, alienated by the superficiality and decadence of Vienna, he wrote in a letter home in October 1908. 'I imagine the Kapuzinerberg has already risen in the blazing red of autumn and the Gaisberg has slipped on a soft gown well suited to its trim figure. The glockenspiel plays "the last rose…," melting into the sober, amicable evening, so tenderly that the heavens arch to infinity! And the song of the fountain drifts so melodiously across the Residenzplatz and the Dom casts her majestic shadows. And the silence rises and roams about the squares and streets. If I could linger with you amidst that splendour, life would go better for me. I don't know if anyone can feel the magic of that city as I do, a magic that saddens the heart with an excess of joy.'

In diefem Haufe
verbrachte der Dichter
GEORG TRAKL
(1887-1914)
feine Kindheit und
Jugend.

Errichtet von der Raimundgefellfchaft zum
75.Geburtstag des Dichters am 3.Februar 1962

A modest plaque on the side of the café Glockenspiel declares that 'In this house the poet Georg Trakl spent his childhood and youth'

Inside one requires a good deal of imagination to see the Trakl family home as it once might have been. The upper floor is one vast space littered with constantly-wiped formica tables where tourists recharge on hot chocolate and strudel as white-aproned waiters whip past with the most cavalier self-assurance. The third window from the left is there for sure but nothing else. We are left only with the view across the square which Trakl would have known so intimately but little more. However, just around the corner on the Waagplatz there is something much more substantial. The birthplace of Trakl, a spacious first floor apartment overlooking the river at its rear and set some way back from the square now forms the 'Trakl Haus' a memorial museum and research foundation run by the dedicated Dr Hans Weichselbaum. One approaches down a cavernous tunnel into an attractive period courtyard containing an ancient stone well and surrounded on two sides by spectacular renaissance style colonnades rising several storeys. In Trakl's day these were enclosed with arched windows of glass and hence their beauty was somewhat

Trakl Haus courtyard

obscured, but after major restoration work during the establishment of the museum the colonnades were returned to their original state. The Trakl Haus itself consists of several rooms, once the living area of the family, containing various Trakl-related items and some original furniture, a small library and archive, as well as an anteroom for showing a film about Trakl's life and work. The most prized possession as Dr Weichselbaum is keen to point out is the self-portrait which Trakl painted in 1912 hanging proudly on the wall of what was once the drawing room. This unsettling image, heavily layered with oils in shades of a deep crimson and purple was famously interfered with at a later date by the wife of the sculptor who then owned it. 'That's not how Trakl looked!' she stridently announced one day and proceeded to daub white paint around the eyes, nose and mouth of the portrait in order to heighten the effect of the ghastly image. The result is, as she had presumably hoped, an altogether more ghoulish apparition.

One of the most precious sites relating to Trakl and which cannot be visited without special permission since it is privately owned, is the little garden on the Pfeifergasse which the young Georg and his sister Greta played in as children. Lacking a garden of their own, Trakl's parents arranged for their children to walk the few hundred yards or so across Mozartplaz to enjoy this borrowed play-

Summer house in the garden on the Pfeifergasse

ground, an old walled garden of fruit trees watched over by the ever faithful Kapuzinerberg. The focus of the garden was and still is the charming wooden summer house which has been lovingly preserved by the present owners. It was here that Trakl chose to pose members of the 'Minerva' literary society, a group of earnest and romantically inclined young men who sought to emulate the decadent French poets they admired. They stand or sit in reflective attitude around a rather refined drawing room table clearly lugged outside for the purpose. It recalls the famous painting by Fantin-Latour 'Coin de table' from 1872 which shows Verlaine and Rimbaud fatefully isolated at the edge of a group in similarly arranged pose. Behind Trakl and his friends stands the summer house, just as it appears today.

M. Mora's bookshop

Moving from the Dom to the Residenzplatz one passes the bookshop M. Mora, whose period frontage immediately draws one to its windows. On entering, the visitor finds an interior which appears to have resisted any modernisation and the aisles, shelves and stairs seem to have gathered into themselves some collective remnant of the souls of those who passed through here. Trakl was one of them. Living only a stone's throw away, he was a regular visitor and many of the books which informed his later poetry were acquired here. One savours the solemn and dignified scent of long preserved wood, such as one finds in old English churches, a hint of varnish perhaps and other materials no longer made nor known. Here, these mysterious aromatic resonances linger on as a trapped atmosphere. Books may come and go and the browsers change but the bookshop remains. The cycle seems so embedded as to be entirely self-sufficient. But each time the door is opened the external world tries to storm in and the precious atmosphere imperceptibly weakens.

St Peter's churchyard

An early poem by Trakl is entitled 'In St Peter's Churchyard'. Beneath the grey, oppressive rock face that rises vertically up towards the fortress on the Mönchsberg nestles the picturesque churchyard of St Peter. This romantic corner of the city is best visited early in the morning or last thing before closure at dusk when the snake of tourists has moved elsewhere. Only then can it be properly appreciated in its true peacefulness and unthreatening melancholy. Cobbled pathways lead around a tiny church and through clusters of tombs bedecked with cast iron ornaments, crosses, figurines and angels. Along the base of the rock wall and filling the recesses carved out of the cliff are little chapels and tombs set behind iron railings. It is not difficult to imagine the lonely Trakl wandering through here at twilight encouraging the sympathetic surroundings to feed his morbid romanticism. 'Rock loneliness is all around. The pale death flowers shudder on graves, which in darkness mourn – yet this mourning knows no pain.'

Unlike in the UK (where poets are merely tolerated as work-shy eccentrics), in Salzburg they are properly appreciated; the authorities have seen fit to erect not only plaques on their poet's former residencies but have also mounted tablets at each location of relevance to the poet engraved with a poem relating to that particular site. For example in the Mirabell Gardens one happens upon another early poem by Trakl 'Music in the Mirabell'. Here tourists will pause as they are inclined to do when something of novelty seizes their eye and then with varying degrees of interest or disinterest read or move on. When I paused to take the following photograph of the poem a group of Japanese visitors nodded excitedly at me and resolved to follow suit. They each in turn took a picture and one even stood next to the poem to be photographed. I had the distinct impression that these cheerful and most amicable souls had no idea whatsoever who Trakl was, why the poem was there or indeed why they had taken the picture other than that they had seen me doing so and therefore imagined such a site of crucial importance to their European tour.

Another important and perhaps unlikely Trakl site is 'The Angel' pharmacy located on Linzergasse, which in Trakl's day was known as 'The White Angel'. He did part of his apprenticeship here

The Angel Pharmacy

when qualifying as a pharmacist and returned to be employed in the dispensary from 1911-12. Such a position gave him easy access to the drugs on which he was relying more and more heavily to maintain an increasingly precarious existence. Suffering acute anxiety from the demands of social contact with the public, Trakl would sweat profusely from his labours and according to legend would get through several shirts a day. It was not long before he found the work intolerable and was forced to leave the premises altogether. Outside passers-by may pause to read the poem 'In Darkness', engraved in perpetuity on the wall beneath the stone bust of the angel.

Naturally many of Trakl's poems will have been inspired by the city and environs of Salzburg without direct reference to them in content or title; 'On the Mönchsberg' is an exception. But it is outside the city one must go to find the location which even now on this November day in 2004 corresponds willingly to Trakl's im-

161

Pond at Hellbrunn with plaque

agery and to which he dedicated two poems. The park at Hellbrunn is still a place of escape for the townspeople of Salzburg and also attracts a steady trickle of international visitors who come to see the famous trick fountains in the grounds of the estate. The gardens of 'Schloss' Hellbrunn, more a country house, retain a special atmosphere. Perhaps the melancholy presence of the three ancient trout ponds which dominate the space have something to do with it. Trakl dedicated an early poem to them and now 'The Three Ponds in Hellbrunn' is suitably displayed on a park building beside one of the ponds. The large rectangular pools secure in their ancient stone are uncannily still and peaceful. Standing at the edge of their brown, listless waters one can imagine how they might have helped to absorb a little of Trakl's anguish. The atmosphere of autumnal decline and peaceful reverie evoked by the poem 'In Hellbrunn' was still much in evidence today. 'Ever shadowing the blue lament of evening / Along the hill, the springtime pond – / As though the shades of those long deceased / The bishops and noblewomen floated over them – / Already their flowers bloom, earnest violets / In evening's abyss, crystal wave of the blue source / Rushing on. With such devotion grow / The greening oaks over the forgotten paths of the dead, / The golden cloud over the pond.'

Hellbrunn

162

Georg Trakl in Innsbruck, May 1914
© *Georg-Trakl-Forschungs-und-Gedenkstätte, Salzburg*

GEORG TRAKL (1887-1914)

In July 1914, just before the outbreak of war, Ludwig Wittgenstein asked the editor of the leading Austrian literary journal *Der Brenner* for the names of two deserving poets on whom he could bestow a generous financial donation from his inheritance. On the advice of the editor, Von Ficker, the money was awarded to the Austrian Georg

Trakl, whose highly expressive visionary poetry had already deeply impressed the other recipient of that award, Rainer Maria Rilke. From a precarious existence and in the space of a few years, Trakl, a veritable *poète maudit*, poured forth an extraordinary and unclassifiable volume of poems replete with mesmerising imagery and haunting visions. Highly sensitive and morbidly introspective, the young poet from Salzburg took his cue from Nietzsche, Rimbaud and Dostoyevsky.

Trakl's preoccupation is the fall of mankind, a yearning for transcendence through religious purity and love in the face of overwhelming morbid despair. Incoherent symbolic images cascade in a delirious fashion to form dream-like worlds, both nightmarish and eerily beautiful. Despite numerous attempts to explain Trakl's vision, his poetry has steadfastly defied any coherent critical analysis. Though Trakl's vision is bleak, there is great tenderness and a sense of hope against all the odds secreted in his poetry, factors which are often overlooked in the light of his brief and irrevocably doomed existence.

In November 1914, Trakl, who had enthusiastically enlisted in the Austrian army as a medical orderly, died from an overdose of cocaine whilst being held for psychiatric observation in a military hospital in Krakow, Poland. He was twenty-seven.

WILL STONE was born in 1966 and lives in Suffolk. He is a poet and translator and holds an MA in Literary Translation from the University of East Anglia. His translation of *Les Chimères* by Gérard de Nerval was published by Menard Press in 1999. He has contributed as editor, translator, essayist and photographer to a new translation of the novel *Bruges-la-Morte* by Belgian

symbolist poet Georges Rodenbach, published by Dedalus in 2005. Further translations of poems by Baudelaire, Nerval, Verhaeren, Rodenbach and Egon Schiele have appeared in various journals including *Modern Poetry in Translation, Poetry Salzburg, Agenda, The International Review* and *Pretext*. His reviews have appeared in the *TLS, Guardian, Independent on Sunday, The London Magazine, Poetry Review* and *PN Review*. A number of his translations were also selected for the Tate anthology of German Expressionist poetry, *Music While Drowning*, in 2003, the title of which is taken from a poem by Schiele. He has published several pamphlet collections of poetry as well as an essay on poet / singer-songwriter Nick Drake. Future projects include a collection of Belgian Symbolist poets in translation and a prose work set in Belgium.

Also available in the Arc Publications
TRANSLATION series
(Translations Editor: Jean Boase-Beier)

ROSE AUSLÄNDER (Germany)
Mother Tongue: Selected Poems
Translated by Jean Boase-Beier & Anthony Vivis

*A Fine Line: New Poetry from Eastern
& Central Europe* (anthology)
EDS. JEAN BOASE-BEIER, ALEXANDRA BÜCHLER, FIONA SAMPSON
Various translators

FRANCO FORTINI (Italy)
Poems
Translated by Michael Hamburger

EVA LIPSKA (Poland)
Pet Shops & Other Poems
Translated by Basia Bogoczek & Tony Howard

Altered State: An Anthology of New Polish Poetry
EDS. ROD MENGHAM, TADEUSZ PIÓRO, PIOTR SZYMOR
Translated by Rod Mengham, Tadeusz Pióro *et al*

CATHAL Ó SEARCAIGH (Ireland)
By the Hearth in Mín a' Leá
Translated by Frank Sewell, Seamus Heaney & Denise Blake

TOMAZ SALAMUN (Slovenia)
Homage to Hat, Uncle Guido and Eliot
Translated by the author, Charles Simic, Anselm Hollo,
Michael Waltuch *et al*

Lightning Source UK Ltd.
Milton Keynes UK
UKOW04f0059090216

267959UK00001B/99/P